||| NEXT ||| MOVE

WORKBOOK

WITH MP3 CD

2

SUZANNE GAYNOR

T0350666

Contents

Starter Unit

Grammar *To be*

1 Choose the correct options.

1 My best friend *is* Spanish.
   a am **(b)** is **c** are

2 The pens .... on the table in my room.
   a am not **b** isn't **c** aren't

3 I .... in an English class.
   a am **b** is **c** are

4 James .... happy today.
   a are **b** aren't **c** isn't

5 .... you in the garden?
   a Am **b** Is **c** Are

6 We .... in the living room.
   a aren't **b** isn't **c** is

2 Complete the conversation.

Max Hi! [1] *My name's* (my name / be) Max.
   [2] .... (you / be) Emily?
Emily Yes, [3] .... (I / be). Hi Max.
Max [4] .... (you / be) German?
Emily No, [5] .... (I / be).
Max [6] .... (this / be) your book?
Emily No, [7] .... (it / be).
Max [8] .... (these / be) your pens?
Emily No, [9] .... (they / be).

Have got

3 Write sentences and questions with the correct form of *have got*.

1 Jack / a new MP3 player. ✔
   Jack has got a new MP3 player.

2 you / a present / for your mother's birthday **?**
   ....

3 she / a black cat ✘
   ....

4 we / a good computer game ✔
   ....

5 they / a big garden ✘
   ....

6 your cousins / a house near the sea **?**
   ....

4 Complete the text with the correct form of *is* or *has got*.

Max [1] *is* a student, but he [2] .... at school today. He [3] .... at home in the living room. He [4] .... ten Maths exercises for homework, but his Maths book [5] .... in his school bag next to him. Max's dog, Bubbles, [6] .... in the living room, too. Bubbles [7] .... a big dog. She [8] .... a very small dog and she [9] .... very short legs. Can you see her? She [10] .... under the chair.

There is/are

5 Write questions and answers with the correct form of *there is/are*.

1 an apple on the table? ✘ (an egg)
  A *Is there an apple on the table?*
  B *No, there isn't. There's an egg on the table.*

2 two cats in the house? ✓ (two big cats)
  A ....
  B ....

3 a bike in the garden? ✓ (a red bike)
  A ....
  B ....

4 two computer games on the desk?
  ✘ (two CDs)
  A ....
  B ....

5 a jacket on the chair? ✘ (a T-shirt)
  A ....
  B ....

6 two windows in the room?
  ✓ (two small windows)
  A ....
  B ....

Personal and Object pronouns

6 Complete the sentences with personal and object pronouns.

1 Hey! That's my book! Give it to *me*!

2 David is my friend and I like ....
  very much.

3 ....'m Emilie and this is Celine.
  ....'re from France.

4 Is Naomi here? This book is for
  ....

5 That's Mr Smith. ....'s a great
  English teacher.

6 That's a great song! Can I listen to
  .... ?

7 Hey, Vanessa! Where are they? I can't see
  ....

8 I've got a sister. ....likes music.

9 Those are my dogs, Oscar and Ben. I love
  ....

10 I like blue. ....'s my favourite
  colour.

Possessive 's

7 Rewrite the sentences. Put apostrophes in the correct places.

1 It's my brothers birthday. He's sixteen.
  It's my brother's birthday. He's sixteen.

2 Lucy is Ralphs sister.
  ....

3 My cousins names are Patrick and Aaron.
  ....

4 These are Lauras bags.
  ....

5 Nicks father is a doctor.
  ....

6 That girls eyes are blue.
  ....

7 The childrens teacher is in the classroom.
  ....

8 The students school bags are on the floor.
  ....

Possessive pronouns

8 Rewrite the sentences with possessive pronouns.

1 My dad's got a big desk.
  His desk is big.

2 I've got a red T-shirt.
  ....

3 We've got a nice teacher.
  ....

4 The cat's got green eyes.
  ....

5 Maria's sister is a doctor.
  ....

6 You've got a nice jacket.
  ....

7 Amy and Liam have got a new computer.
  ....

8 I've got a great magazine!
  ....

Vocabulary Places

1 Look at the pictures. Complete the words.

park

m........................

r........................

l........................

c........................

c........................

s........................

z........................

2 Choose the correct options.

1 Max and Emily are at the train *station,* but they haven't got their tickets.
   a café **(b)** station **c** centre

2 'I want a coffee and a sandwich.'
   'Let's go to the .... .'
   a museum **b** café **c** library

3 I want to buy a T-shirt from the shop in the .... .
   a library **b** shopping centre **c** station

4 There's a new swimming pool at the .... .
   a library **b** cinema **c** sports centre

5 We want to see the elephants at the .... .
   a zoo **b** museum **c** shopping centre

6 In the .... you can play football.
   a library **b** museum **c** park

Possessions

3 Complete the crossword.

```
¹W A T ²C H        ³        ⁴
              ⁵
      ⁶    ⁷
      ⁸        ⁹
¹⁰
        ¹¹
```

Across

①

⑤

⑥

⑧

⑩

⑪

Down

②

③

④

⑦

⑧

⑨

Countries and Nationalities

4 Complete the puzzle and find the mystery country.

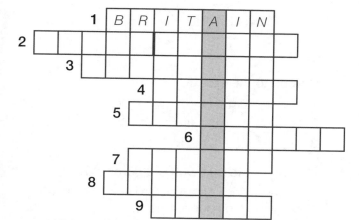

1 B R I T A I N
2
3
4
5
6
7
8
9

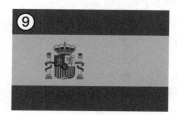

5 Complete the sentences.

1 Samantha is from Britain. She's *British*.
2 Kurt is from Germany. He's ....
3 Mandy is from the USA. She's ....
4 Rosa is from Italy. She's ....
5 Vasily is from Russia. He's ....
6 Paulo is from Portugal. He's ....
7 Carmen is from Spain. She's ....
8 Alexis is from Greece. He's ....

6 Complete the text with these words.

British	centre	~~fifteen~~	France
jeans	park	shopping	T-shirt

Hi. My name's Sandrine and I'm [1] *fifteen* years old. I'm from [2] .... but my family and I don't live there. We live in London and I've got lots of [3] .... friends. I love London. Our house is near a fantastic [4] .... and there is also a sports [5] .... with a swimming pool.

That's me in the photo. Today I've got my favourite [6] .... and blue [7] .... on. Do you like them? They're from a great shop at my favourite [8] .... centre. London is a great place for fashion!

1 Play The Game!

Vocabulary Sports

★ **1** Look at the pictures. Complete the crossword with the sports.

| ¹G | Y | M | N | A | ²S | T | I | C | S |

Crossword grid with entries numbered 3, 4, 5, 6, 7, 8.

Across

Down

★ **2** Complete the sports.

1 ba <u>s</u> <u>k</u> <u>e</u> tb <u>a</u> <u>l</u> <u>l</u>
2 h _ _ s _ -r _ d _ _ g
3 m _ _ n _ _ _ n b _ k _ _ _
4 i _ e h _ c _ _ y
5 ic_-sk _ _ _ _ _
6 f _ _ _ b _ l _

★★ **3** Complete the text with *do, go* or *play*.

Adam and Vince ¹*play* football every weekend. Their sister Judy doesn't ².......................... football – she doesn't like it – but she and her friends ³.......................... tennis on Saturdays. They also ⁴.......................... athletics at school and they want to take part in the Olympic Games one day. In the Christmas holidays, Adam, Vince and Judy ⁵.......................... snowboarding and their parents ⁶.......................... skiing. In the summer holidays they all ⁷.......................... mountain biking. Next year the children want to start a new sport, Adam wants to ⁸.......................... judo, Vince wants to ⁹.......................... archery and Judy wants to ¹⁰.......................... horse-riding.

★★ **4** Write sentences with *do, go* and *play*.

1 we / swimming in summer / judo in winter
We go swimming in summer and do judo in winter.

2 Beth and Mark / basketball on Mondays / ice-skating at the weekend
....

3 I / athletics at school / skateboarding in the park
....

4 they / horse-riding every day / tennis on Saturdays
....

5 Sam and Billy / gymnastics / football at school
....

6 we / ice hockey in winter / mountain biking in summer
....

Vocabulary page 104

Reading

★ **1** Look at the photo. Which sport is the interview about?

a Skiing b Ice-skating c Ice hockey

> **Brain Trainer**
>
> **Underline these words in the text:**
>
> 1 Olympic sport 4 other sports
> 2 easy 5 swim
> 3 want 6 night
>
> **Now do Exercise 2.**

★ **2** Read the interview. Answer the questions.

1 Is ice-skating an Olympic sport? *Yes, it is.*
2 Is it an easy sport? ....
3 What do Martin and Madeleine want to do one day? ....
4 Do they do other sports? ....
5 Can Martin swim? ....
6 What time do Madeleine and Martin go to bed at night? ....

★★ **3** Read the interview again. Are the sentences true (T), false (F) or don't know (DK)?

1 Madeleine and Martin practise ice-skating for two hours on school days. *F*
2 They practise ice-skating once a day at the weekend. ....
3 Martin likes his dance lessons. ....
4 Madeleine talks about ice-skating and two other sports. ....
5 Martin doesn't like the sea. ....
6 Madeleine and Martin's friends do their homework before school. ....

★★ **4** Complete the sentences.

1 Madeleine and Martin practise for *fifteen* hours a week on school days.
2 They practise for .... hours every week.
3 Good ice-skaters can move well on the ice because they can ....
4 In the mornings Madeleine and Martin have .... before they do their ....
5 In the holidays Madeleine goes .... but Martin goes ....

Cool sports!

In *Teen Sports* this week, James Biggs interviews twins Madeleine and Martin Rogers. Their favourite sport? Ice-skating.

James	Madeleine, most young people do sports like athletics, swimming or tennis. Why is ice-skating your favourite sport?
Madeleine	Because it's so beautiful.
James	But is it really a sport?
Martin	Yes, it's an Olympic sport and it isn't easy! Madeleine and I practise every day after school for three hours. And at the weekend we practise for two hours in the morning and two hours in the evening. We want to win an Olympic medal one day.
Madeleine	We also have dance lessons once a week because ice-skaters must move well on the ice.
James	Do you do any other sports?
Madeleine	Well, I do gymnastics at school, and in the holidays I go swimming. I love the sea but Martin hates the water.
Martin	That's right. I can't swim, so I don't go with Madeleine. I go mountain biking instead.
James	So when do you find time to eat and sleep and do your homework?
Martin	It's difficult. We get up at five every morning – two hours before our friends! Then we have breakfast and do our homework before school.
Madeleine	We can't do our homework at night because we're tired. We go to bed at nine.
James	That's a long day! Well, thank you for speaking to me and good luck in the next Olympics!

Grammar Present simple

★ 1 **Choose the correct options.**

1 James *play /(plays)* basketball at school on Monday.
2 He *don't / doesn't* do judo every day.
3 *Do / Does* they go mountain biking at the weekend?
4 We *don't / doesn't* play tennis every Thursday.
5 What ball games does Julia *play / plays* at school?
6 I *watch / watches* football on TV.

★ 2 **Look at the table. Match the questions (1–6) with the answers (a–f).**

	Liam	Sarah	Melissa
go swimming	✓	✗	✗
play hockey	✓	✗	✓
go snowboarding	✓	✓	✓
do athletics	✗	✗	✗

1 Does Liam go snowboarding?   *d*
2 Do Sarah and Melissa do athletics?
3 Does Liam do athletics?
4 Does Sarah go snowboarding?
5 Do Liam and Melissa play hockey?
6 Does Sarah go swimming?

a No, he doesn't.
b Yes, she does.
c Yes, they do.
d Yes, he does.
e No, they don't.
f No, she doesn't.

★★ 3 **Look at the table in Exercise 2 again. Complete the sentences with the Present simple form of the verbs.**

1 Liam and Melissa *don't do* (do) athletics.
2 Melissa .... (play) hockey.
3 Sarah .... (go) swimming.
4 Liam and Sarah .... (go) snowboarding.
5 Sarah .... (do) athletics.
6 Sarah and Melissa .... (go) swimming.

★★ 4 **Write questions and answers in the Present simple.**

1 your friends / play / basketball after school? ✓
   A *Do your friends play basketball after school?*
   B *Yes, they do.*
2 you / go / mountain biking / at the weekend? ✗
   A ....
   B ....
3 your sister / like / team sports? ✓
   A ....
   B ....
4 you / practise / a sport / on Fridays? ✓
   A ....
   B ....
5 your brother / watch TV / every day? ✗
   A ....
   B ....

★★ 5 **Complete the email with the Present simple form of the verbs.**

New Message

Hi Matt,

I [1] *love* (love) it here and Helen [2] .... (love) it, too. We [3] .... (not want) to go back to England! Australia is a great country. The weather is fantastic and Helen and I [4] .... (go) swimming at the beach every day. Mum and Dad [5] .... (come) with us, but Dad [6] .... (not go) in the water. He can't swim! What [7] .... (he / do)? Well, he [8] .... (sit) under an umbrella all day and [9] .... (read) a newspaper!

Write soon.
James

Send

Add Attachments:

Verb + -ing

★ 6 Complete the sentences.

love: 😊😊	like/enjoy: 😊	don't mind: 😐
don't like: 🙁	hate: 🙁🙁	

1 Emma 😐 *doesn't mind* staying at home.
2 Cathy 😊 .... going running.
3 .... you 😊 .... watching the Olympic Games on TV?
4 I 😊😊 .... going skateboarding.
5 Andrea 🙁🙁 .... swimming.
6 Dad 😐 .... watching athletics.
7 I 🙁 .... getting up early.
8 .... Eddie 😐 .... doing athletics?

★ 7 Complete the sentences with the -ing form of the verbs.

1 We love *watching* (watch) football matches on TV.
2 They don't like .... (do) judo at school.
3 Why does Amy hate .... (play) ice hockey?
4 The boys don't mind .... (take) me with them to the sports centre.
5 Do you enjoy .... (swim) in cold water?
6 Mum doesn't like .... (go) horse-riding.

★ 8 Write sentences.

1 Helen and Nick / 😊 / play / tennis
Helen and Nick like playing tennis.

2 my brother / 😊😊 / watch / the Olympic Games / on TV!
....

3 we / 🙁🙁 / swim / in the sea
....

4 Sonia / 😐 / practise / every day
....

5 David / 😊 / snowboarding / in winter?
....

6 I / 🙁 / do / my homework / at the weekend
....

Grammar Reference pages 86–87

Vocabulary Compound nouns

★ 1 Match 1–6 to a–f to make compound nouns.

1 football	a skates
2 tennis	b stick
3 hockey	c racket
4 judo	d costume
5 ice	e belt
6 swimming	f boots

★ 2 Complete the sentences with these words.

~~court~~	court	pitch	pool	rink	track

1 I play basketball at the basketball *court*.
2 She doesn't like swimming at the swimming ....
3 Do you go ice-skating at the new ice-skating .... ?
4 They do athletics at the new athletics ....
5 We play football on the football ....
6 He plays tennis on this tennis ....

★★ 3 Complete the sentences with these words.

athletics	~~boots~~	court	judo
pitch	pool	stick	tennis

1 It's football practice after school. Please take your football *boots* with you.
2 She's a great athlete. She goes to the .... track every day.
3 I haven't got a .... racket.
4 Please meet me at the football ....
5 What colour .... belt have you got?
6 You can't play ice hockey! You haven't got a hockey ....
7 There are ten players on the basketball ....
8 Let's go to the swimming ....

★★ 4 Complete the text.

On Mondays Rachel plays ice hockey and she takes her [1] *hockey stick* with her. On Wednesdays she does judo. She's very good and she's got a green [2] .... On Fridays she does athletics and she practises at the [3] ....
On Saturday mornings she puts on her tennis clothes. Then she takes her [4] .... and goes to the [5] .... In the afternoons she goes ice-skating at the [6] .... She loves this sport.

Vocabulary page 104

Chatroom Opinions

Speaking and Listening

★ **1** Complete the sentences with these words.

do favourite ~~it~~ like of think

1 I can't play tennis! That's *it*! I quit!
2 What do you think .... my new tennis racket?
3 Mrs Marshall is my .... teacher.
4 I don't .... going to the ice-skating rink. It's boring.
5 I .... Usain Bolt is amazing.
6 .... you like watching the Olympic Games on TV?

★ **2** ◎ 1.2 Match the questions (1–5) to the answers (a–e). Then listen and check.

1 What do you think of England? *c*
2 Do you like watching archery?
3 What do you think of Usain Bolt?
4 Do you like Rihanna?
5 What do you think of Arsenal?

a He's my favourite athlete. I think he's amazing!
b I think they're good, but Chelsea are my favourite team.
c Well, I think the weather is terrible, but I like the people.
d Yes, I do. I think it's an amazing sport.
e No, I don't. Beyoncé is my favourite singer.

★★ **3** ◎ 1.3 Complete the conversation with these phrases. Then listen and check.

Do you like	~~Good idea~~
I don't like	I love
I think	Nadal is my favourite player
What do you think	

Carlos	Do you want to watch tennis on TV?
Zak	[1] *Good idea!*
Carlos	What about you, Nadia?
Nadia	Sorry, Carlos. [2] .... tennis is boring.
Carlos	Really? I love it. [3] .... of Roger Federer, Zak?
Zak	I think he's good, but [4] ....
Jody	My favourite sport is horse-riding. I go horse-riding every weekend.
Zak	[5] .... horses, Nadia?
Nadia	Yes, I do. [6] .... them. I can't ride but I want to learn.
Jody	Do you? What about you, Zak?
Zak	No thanks! [7] .... horses.

★★ **4** Read the conversation in Exercise 3 again. Are the sentences true (T), false (F) or don't know (DK)?

1 Zak wants to watch tennis with Carlos. T
2 Nadia doesn't like tennis. ....
3 Roger Federer is Jody's favourite player. ....
4 Jody likes horse-riding. ....
5 Nadia goes horse-riding every weekend. ....
6 Zak doesn't want to go horse-riding. ....

★★★ **5** Look at the table and write a conversation between Andy and Eva. Use the information below and expressions from Exercise 3.

	Likes	Doesn't like
Andy	playing football listening to music watching TV	reading books shopping cooking
Eva	swimming reading books playing computer games	watching TV getting up early cooking

Speaking and Listening page 113

Grammar Adverbs of frequency

★ 1 Complete the table with these adverbs of frequency.

always	hardly ever	~~never~~
often	~~sometimes~~	usually

☆☆☆☆ *never*
★☆☆☆ _____
★★☆☆ *sometimes* / _____
★★★☆ _____
★★★★ _____

Brain Trainer

Draw pictures to help you remember words.

1 ⚽ ⚽ ⚽ usually
2 ⚽ hardly ever

Now do Exercise 2.

★ 2 Look at the table. Complete the sentences.

	Naomi	Jake	Harry	Isobel
go swimming on Tuesdays	🥽🥽🥽	–	🥽🥽🥽🥽	🥽🥽
do homework after school	📚📚📚	📚📚	–	📚📚
watch TV at the weekend	📺	📺📺	📺	–

1 Naomi *usually* goes swimming on Tuesdays.
2 Harry .... does his homework after school.
3 Harry and Naomi .... watch TV at the weekend.
4 Isobel .... goes swimming on Tuesdays.
5 Jake and Isobel .... do their homework after school.
6 Jake .... goes swimming on Tuesdays.
7 Isobel .... watches TV at the weekend.

★★ 3 Rewrite the sentences with the adverbs of frequency in the correct place.

1 We play tennis on Saturday afternoons. (always)
We always play tennis on Saturday afternoons.

2 Julia goes skateboarding with her friends at the weekend. (sometimes)
....
....

3 I meet my friends at the sports centre after school. (often)
....
....

4 I wear a football shirt at home. (hardly ever)
....

5 Sam takes his tennis racket to school. (never)
....
....

6 I am happy at the weekend. (usually)
....
....

★★ 4 Write sentences and questions.

1 we / always / not get up / late at the weekend
We don't always get up late at the weekend.

2 I / sometimes / be / tired / in the evening
....

3 he / often / cook / dinner / for his family?
....

4 our teacher / hardly ever / give / us / tests
....

5 you / usually / meet / your friends / after school?
....

6 I / not / always / watch / football / on Saturdays
....

★★ 5 Answer the questions.

1 What do you always do in the evening?
I always listen to music.

2 What do you and your friends usually do at the weekend?
....

3 What do you sometimes do on holiday?
....

4 What sports do you hardly ever watch on TV?
....

5 What do you never do?
....

Grammar Reference pages 86–87

Reading

1 Read the article quickly. Find:

  1 one country   *France*
  2 two people   ....
  3 a film   ....
  4 four sports   ....
  5 two places in a town   ....

IT'S FAST, IT'S EXCITING – IT'S FREE RUNNING!

Free running is an exciting new sport from France but it has fans all over the world. You don't usually see free runners at athletics tracks. You see them in the street or in parks. They climb walls, jump from building to building and do a lot of other amazing movements. It is important to move fast but it is also important to move beautifully.

Good free runners practise every day. They don't wear special clothes but good running shoes are important. Free runners sometimes run with their MP3 players and they listen to their favourite music.

Free running is a difficult sport but it's very popular with teenagers. Free runner Robbie Dowling, 17, says 'Free running is different from sports like athletics, football or judo. When I go free running, I don't want to win or lose; I just want to have fun. Sure, there are competitions, but they aren't important to me or my friends. We don't take part in them.'

For other young people, free running competitions are important and you can watch some amazing videos on YouTube. You can also watch Sébastien Foucan, the man who started the sport, free running in the James Bond film, *Casino Royale*. Sébastien says that free runners practise all the time. He also says there is no good or bad in free running, but it is important to learn from your experiences.

2 Read the article again. Choose the correct options.

  1 People all over the world (enjoy) / don't enjoy free running.
  2 Free runners usually practise *in the street / at an athletics track*.
  3 *All / Some* free runners practise every day.
  4 Free runners don't wear *special shoes / special clothes*.
  5 Robbie Dowling wants *to win / doesn't enter* free running competitions.
  6 You can watch free running competitions *on YouTube / in the film Casino Royale*.

3 Complete the summary with words from the article.

Free running is a sport with ¹ *fans* all over the world. Free runners usually run in the ².......................... or in parks. Some people go free running because they want to have ³.......................... . Other people like taking part in ⁴.........................., but there is no good or ⁵.......................... in free running. It's a great sport!

Listening

1 ◗◗ 1.4 Listen to the radio show about sports clothes. Tick the words you hear.

  sports centre ☐
  football shirts ☐
  football boots ☐
  ice hockey ☐
  tennis racket ☐
  running shoes ☐

2 ◗◗ 1.4 Listen again. Choose the correct options.

  1 Mark (always) / sometimes wears football shirts.
  2 He *likes / doesn't like* playing football.
  3 *Football / Ice hockey* is Mark's favourite sport.
  4 Elena *loves / hates* wearing running shoes.
  5 She *always / never* wears football shirts.

Writing A description of a sport

1 Match 1–5 to a–e.

1 comma   a **!**
2 full stop   b **'**
3 question mark   c **,**
4 apostrophe   d **?**
5 exclamation mark   e **.**

2 Put the correct punctuation in the sentences.

1 *At school, we play football, basketball and tennis.*
2 Do you enjoy playing tennis with your friends
3 I dont like watching ice hockey on TV but I love playing it
4 Lionel Messi is an amazing player He's great
5 This is Lucys sisters judo belt
6 Are there ten or eleven people in a football team

3 Read the text. Match the questions (1–3) to the paragraphs (A–C).

1 What's my favourite sport at school?   ....
2 What do I think of sport at school?   ....
3 What sports are there at school?   .A.

4 Think about sports at your school. Complete the sentences.

1 Sport at school is ....
2 At my school, there's ....
3 My favourite sport is ....
4 We play ....
5 I think sport at school is ....

5 Write a description of sport at your school. Use the paragraph guide from Exercise 3 and your sentences from Exercise 4.

....
....
....
....
....
....
....
....
....
....
....

Sport at school

A Sport at my school is amazing. There's tennis, basketball, football and athletics. We sometimes go swimming in the swimming pool. My friends love tennis and they play every day. I hardly ever play tennis because I don't like it. I think it's difficult.

B My favourite sport is basketball. I think it's an exciting sport and I play in the school basketball team. We play basketball every Monday and Wednesday and there are matches every week. We aren't very good and we usually lose, but we have fun!

C I think sport at school is great. I love playing in a team with my friends. It's never boring.

Vocabulary Types of films

★ **1** Complete the film words.

1 h o r r o r f i l m
2 m _ _ i _ a _
3 d _ _ u _ e _ t _ r _
4 a _ t _ _ n f _ l _
5 _ _ m _ d _
6 s _ _ _ _ _ e f _ _ _ _ o _ _ _ lm
7 f _ _ _ _ _ y
8 m _ _ _ ial a _ _ _ f _ _ m
9 a _ _ m _ _ _ d f _ _ _
10 we _ _ e _ _
11 w _ r _ _ lm
12 h _ _ t _ _ ic _ _ _ _ lm

★★ **2** Complete the sentences with the correct film words.

1 This is Dan's favourite *comedy*. He loves the jokes.
2 I don't like this m...................... . The songs are boring.
3 The alien and the boy are friends. It's a good s...................... f...................... f...................... .
4 We're making an a...................... f...................... . Look at my cartoons!
5 The d...................... is about snakes. It's interesting and I'm learning a lot.
6 The m...................... a...................... f...................... was good. I love judo and karate!

Vocabulary page 105

★★ **3** Write sentences.

1 she / like / action films
   She likes action films.
2 we / not enjoy / horror films
   ....
3 I / not like / this documentary
   ....
4 you / watch / musicals?
   ....
5 he / never / watch / animated films
   ....
6 they / not like / science fiction films
   ....

★★★ **4** Complete the text with these words.

comedies	historical films	horror films
musicals	~~science fiction films~~	westerns

My family and I love going to the cinema but we don't like the same kinds of films. Mum likes
[1] *science fiction films* because she loves stories about the future. Dad is a fan of [2]...................... .
He enjoys scary stories about vampires. My little sister likes [3]...................... ! She says she likes stories about cowboys, but I think she watches these films because there are usually horses in them. She loves horses. I like [4]......................
because I like laughing, and I love
[5]...................... because the songs in them are often great. I also enjoy [6]...................... about kings and queens.

Reading

Brain Trainer

Look at the pictures. They often help you understand a text.

Now do Exercise 1.

★ **1** Read the magazine article quickly. Match the people (1–5) to the pictures (a–e).

1 Anna .....d.....
2 Frank .....
3 Rachel .....
4 Tanya .....
5 Tom .....

Fantastic Film Club

The best club for thirteen- to sixteen-year-olds at our school is the Film Club. It's got fifty-one members and we meet every Saturday. We usually watch films together and talk about them afterwards. What do we watch? Comedies, action films, historical films, war films and many other types of films. I like fantasies and *The Lord of the Rings* films are my favourites.

Every year the members of the club do a big project. This year we are doing something special: we're making a musical about a school in New York.

Today is Saturday 16th January and we're all at the club. We're working hard because we want to start filming in two months. Rachel and Tom are over there. Rachel is writing the music for the musical. Her job is difficult because there are a lot of songs in the musical. Tom is next to her. He's writing the story for the film and he and Rachel work together. They're important people in this project.

What are the other people doing? Well, Anna is doing the special effects. In the story, there's a storm in New York and Anna is making storm noises on her computer. Are the actors acting? No, they aren't. They're listening to Tanya. She's singing one of Rachel's songs and Frank is playing the piano. They're amazing. This is going to be a great musical!

★ **2** Read the text again. Choose the correct options.

1 The members of the Film Club do a project every (year) / Saturday.
2 They often *watch / make* films and talk about them.
3 The writer's favourite films are *musicals / fantasies*.
4 The members want to start *writing / filming* the musical in two months.
5 The writer *likes / doesn't like* Tanya's singing.

★★ **3** Match the sentence beginnings (1–5) to the endings (a–f).

1 About fifty people are   *f*
2 The writer's favourite films are
3 This year the Film Club is making a film about
4 Tom and Rachel are important because they are writing
5 The actors are listening to
6 The writer thinks Frank is

a the story and the music.
b a school in New York.
c fantasies.
d a good piano player.
e one of Rachel's songs.
f in the Film Club.

★★★ **4** Answer the questions.

1 What do the club members usually do on Saturdays?
They usually watch films and talk about them afterwards.
2 What do they do every year?
....
....
3 What do they want to do in March?
....
....
4 Why is Rachel's job difficult?
....
....
5 What kind of special effects is Anna doing at the moment?
....
....

Grammar Present continuous

★ 1 Complete the sentences with the Present continuous form of the verbs.

1 Sylvia *is watching* (watch) TV.
2 The boys .... (dance) in the musical.
3 We .... tennis (not play) at the moment.
4 He .... (swim) in the pool.
5 I .... (study) for a test right now.
6 She .... (not look) at us.
7 I .... (not wait) for Anna. I .... (wait) for Mike.

★ 2 Choose the correct options.

1 (Are) / Is they writing songs? Yes, they (are) / is.
2 Are / Is Ben acting? No, he aren't / isn't.
3 Are / Is you making a film? Yes, I am / are.
4 Are / Is we buying the tickets? No, we aren't / isn't.
5 Are / Is they studying? No, they aren't / isn't.

★★ 3 Look at the picture. Make sentences with the Present continuous.

1 Amy / not sing – she / dance
   Amy isn't singing. She's dancing.
2 Jake / not run – he / sit
   ....
3 Billy and Leona / not watch Amy – they / talk
   ....
4 Kate and Anna / not laugh – they / dance
   ....
5 the / director / not smile – she / watch / Ben
   ....
6 Lucy / not talk / to the director – she / talk / on her mobile phone
   ....
   ....

Grammar Reference pages 88–89

★★ 4 Look at the picture again. Make questions and answers.

1 what / Ben / do?
   What is Ben doing? He's running.
2 Amy / study?
   ....
3 Billy and Leona / sing?
   ....
4 Lucy / laugh?
   ....
5 what / Jake / do?
   ....
6 who / the director / watch?
   ....

★★★ 5 Imagine you are at home with your family in the evening. What are you and your family doing? Write five sentences.

I'm not watching TV. I'm doing my homework. Mum isn't …

Vocabulary Adjectives

★ **1** Find twelve adjectives.

E	S	I	D	V	X	G	A	D	Y	N
C	R	A	G	F	U	N	N	Y	R	F
I	U	H	D	J	L	I	L	E	A	Z
T	B	T	A	S	T	Y	E	X	C	Q
N	B	S	U	A	Y	O	B	C	S	W
A	I	E	X	P	E	N	S	I	V	E
M	S	B	O	R	I	N	G	T	C	I
O	H	T	E	I	N	A	D	I	S	R
R	B	R	I	L	L	I	A	N	T	D
U	O	K	O	V	D	Z	R	G	D	H

★ **2** Match these words to the pictures.

annoying	boring	exciting
~~expensive~~	romantic	rubbish

expensive

....

....

....

....

....

★★ **3** Put the letters in the correct order.

1 Max loves telling jokes. He's *funny*.   nunfy

2 This ice cream is great. It's very
....   ttsay

3 I love this film! It's .... !   railtlbin

4 I don't understand the story. It's
....   edrwi

5 The horror film is about zombies. It's
....   arsyc

6 People always cry when they watch the film.
It's very ....   dsa

★★ **4** Complete the text with adjectives from Exercise 1. More than one option is possible for some spaces.

It's Saturday evening. Charlie and his family want to see a film. They don't want to go to the cinema because the tickets are [1] *expensive*. They want to eat some [2] .... pizza and watch a DVD, but which one? The action film is [3] .... , but Charlie doesn't want to watch it again. He wants to watch a [4] .... film, but his mum and dad don't like comedies. Charlie's dad says the war film is [5] .... and he wants to watch it, but Charlie's mum says it's [6] .... The horror film is good but it's very [7] .... and Charlie's little sister is only five. There's a documentary about animals but Charlie's grandma doesn't want to watch it. She says documentaries are [8] ....

Vocabulary page 105

Speaking and Listening

★ 1 Put the words in the correct order.

1 A (we / don't / later / Why / go / to the cinema / ?)
Why don't we go to the cinema later?

B (way / No / !) *No way!* I've got a test tomorrow.

2 A (a / Let's / horror film / watch)

....

B (in / I'm / !) .... I love horror films.

3 A (What / computer game / playing / this / about / ?)

....

B (idea / That / good / 's / a) ....
I love games like this.

★ 2 🔊 1.5 **Complete the conversations with these words. Then listen and check.**

about	don't	~~go~~	going
I'm	let's	way	why

1 A Let's ¹*go* for a walk in the park.
B No, thanks! It's raining!

2 A ² .... don't we go for a walk in the park?
B That's a good idea. It's a beautiful day.

3 A What about ³ .... for a walk in the park?
B ⁴ .... in. We can go skateboarding there.

4 A ⁵ .... make dinner for Mum and Dad tonight.
B That's a good idea.

5 A What ⁶ .... making dinner for Mum and Dad tonight?
B No ⁷ .... ! I can't cook!

6 A Why ⁸ .... we make dinner for Mum and Dad tonight?
B OK. We can make them some chicken.

★★ 3 🔊 1.6 **Complete the conversation with these phrases. Then listen and check.**

a good idea	I'm in	let's see
no thanks	what about meeting	~~why don't we~~

Carlos What are you doing, Nadia?
Nadia I'm reading a book about old films. It's interesting.
Jody Well, ¹*why don't we* go to the cinema? *Casablanca* is on at Cinema World.
Nadia Great! ² .... !
Zak *Casablanca?*
Nadia It's an old black and white film. It's very romantic!
Zak ³ .... ! Those films are boring!
Carlos Zak's right. ⁴ .... the new comedy.
Jody Well, ⁵ .... outside the cinema? You and Zak can see the comedy and Nadia and I can see *Casablanca*.
Carlos That's ⁶ ....

★★ 4 Read the conversation in Exercise 3 again. Answer the questions.

1 Why is Nadia reading a book about old films?
It's interesting.

2 Does Zak know what type of film *Casablanca* is?
....

3 What is Zak's opinion of old black and white films?
....

4 What does Carlos want to see?
....

5 What does Carlos think of Jody's suggestion?
....

★★ 5 You and your friends want to do something interesting today. Write a conversation and make suggestions. You can use your own ideas or the ideas below.

You	go to the beach / play tennis
Friend 1	go to the swimming pool / go to the cinema
Friend 2	go skiing / have a party

Grammar Present simple and Present continuous

★ **1** Complete the sentences with the Present simple or Present continuous form of the verbs.

1 I *usually take* (usually / take) black and white photographs, but at the moment I *am taking* (take) colour pictures.

2 Anna .... (usually / not make) documentaries. This year she .... (work) on a horror film.

3 You .... (usually / read) a book on the bus, but today you .... (not read). You .... (listen) to your MP3 player.

4 Emily and Alice .... (usually / not read) sport magazines, but today they .... (read) about football. They .... (not read) about music.

5 Mark .... (usually / work) in his dad's shop after school, but this afternoon he .... (not help) his dad. He .... (play) tennis with his friends.

6 We .... (usually / have) a dance class on Fridays, but this Friday we .... (watch) a DVD at my house.

★ **2** Match the questions (1–10) to the answers (a–j).

1 Is Tessa working in her Mum's shop today?   e
2 Does Jimmy take photos with his phone?
3 Are you and your friend doing your homework?
4 Do the friends often go to the cinema?
5 Are you watching the horror film on TV?
6 Do you and Nick always play tennis together?
7 Does Tessa help her mother in the shop?
8 Is Jimmy taking photographs of the people at the party?
9 Do you often watch DVDs at home?
10 Are your parents having breakfast?

a   No, he isn't.
b   Yes, we are.
c   No, I don't.
d   Yes, I am.
e   Yes, she is.
f   No, they don't.
g   Yes, he does.
h   Yes, we do.
i   Yes, they are.
j   Yes, she does.

★★ **3** Complete the text with the Present simple or Present continuous form of the verbs.

Hi Anna.

I'm in Paris at a school for dancers and I
[1] *'m having* (have) a great time! I usually
[2] .... (go) to dance classes in the mornings but today is Saturday and I
[3] .... (sit) in a café in Montmartre and I [4] .... (write) this postcard.
At the weekend I sometimes [5] .... (meet) my French friends in the evening and we
[6] .... (watch) a good film at the cinema. My best friend here is Emilie and we often
[7] .... (do) things together but at the moment she [8] .... (visit) her grandma.
Write soon,
Samantha

★★ **4** Make sentences in the Present simple and Present continuous.

1 She usually / work / in a café after school / but / she / do / her homework / today
She usually works in a café after school, but she is doing her homework today.

2 I / often / take / photographs / but / I / not use / my camera / right now
....

3 Alice / hardly ever / do / sport / but / she / do / athletics / at the moment
....

4 Max / play / basketball / at the weekend / but / he / not play / today
....

5 Lucy / usually / sit / with Adam / but/ she / sit / with me / today
....

6 our cousins / sometimes / visit / us / at the weekend / but today / we / visit them
....

★★★ **5** Make sentences.

1 usually / at the moment
I usually do homework after school but I'm watching TV at the moment.
I _____

2 every day / today
My friends _____

3 sometimes / now
Mum and Dad _____

Grammar Reference pages 88–89

Reading

Brain Trainer

Don't answer the questions too quickly! Sometimes all the answer options are in the reading text. Read the text carefully!

Now do Exercise 1.

1 Read the festival blog quickly. Where is Anke from?

a the USA   b Germany   c Japan

FilmClub.netcom

HOME   NEWS   BLOG   FEATURES

International Student Film Festival!

Today is the beginning of the International Student Film Festival in Rome and it's an exciting day for the young people here. There are students from the United States, Europe and Japan. One of them is Anke Muller, from Germany. Anke is a seventeen-year-old student and she's staying with friends in Italy this summer. She's taking part in the festival for the first time.

'Animated films are my favourite and I love the Wallace and Gromit films,' she says. 'Some of the characters in these films are really weird, but they're all brilliant, and Gromit, the dog, is very funny.'

Anke loves watching films and she also makes animated films about funny people. 'I love watching people in the street, in the park, at school,' she says. 'They often do weird things.'

Anke makes her films at home. 'My film studio is my bedroom' she says. 'I sit there every day and I make the scenes and characters.' It isn't always easy for Anke. 'I don't have a lot of free time because I often have a lot of homework. I love making films but I don't always like doing my homework!'

This festival is great for Anke because she's with new friends. They can watch films and talk to film directors. Anke's favourite film at the festival is a science fiction film called *The Robot Returns*. 'It's very scary,' says Anke, 'but the special effects are amazing.'

2 Read the blog again. Answer the questions.

1 How old is Anke?
She's seventeen years old.

2 Where is she staying this summer?
....

3 What is her opinion of the characters in the Wallace and Gromit films?
....

4 What kind of film does she make?
....

5 What are her films about?
....

6 What is Anke's favourite film at the festival?
....

3 Complete the summary with words from the article.

Anke Muller is a student. She [1] *is staying* with friends in Italy this summer and she [2] .... in a film festival in Rome. Anke loves watching films and she also [3] .... animated films about funny people. It isn't easy because she hasn't usually got a lot of [4] .... Her favourite film at the festival is a science fiction film. Anke thinks the [5] .... in this film are very good.

Listening

1  **1.7** Read the message. Then listen to Laura and Adam. Who is going to the cinema? Tick the correct option.

a Laura   ....   b Adam   ....

HI FROM CINEMA WORLD!

Get your free tickets for *The Robot Returns* on Saturday.
Phone now on 06849 ....

2 **1.7** Listen again. Are the sentences true (T), false (F) or don't know (DK)?

1 Adam's got a text message from Cinema World.   *F*

2 Laura doesn't usually watch action films.   ....

3 Laura wants to see the film on Sunday.   ....

4 Adam plays basketball on Sunday.   ....

5 Kate wants to go to the cinema with Laura.   ....

Writing A film review

1 Read the film review. Find *and*, *but* and *because*.

Streetdance 3D — A great film!

(A) I love the film *StreetDance 3D*. It's a musical and a love story. I like watching the DVD with my friends because we're students at a dance school.

(B) *StreetDance 3D* is about a group of young dancers. In the film, they are practising for a big dance competition. The group loses an important dancer but they don't stop practising. They want to win.

(C) The film has got interesting characters. My favourite is Carly because she is funny and she can dance. I also like Helena, a teacher at a ballet school. Eddie is another great character. He's a brilliant dancer. All the dancers wear cool clothes and the special effects are amazing.

(D) I think *StreetDance 3D* is a great film because the story is exciting and the music is special.

2 Complete the sentences with *and, but* or *because*.

1 I like the film *because* it has great music.
2 The special effects are good, ... the actors are rubbish.
3 We want to go shopping .... meet our friends on Saturday morning.
4 She can't make dinner .... she can't cook.
5 I often go to the sports centre, ... I never play football there.
6 I don't like the musical .... the story is weird, ... the songs are good.

3 Read the review again. Answer the questions.

1 What kind of film is it?
....
2 What is it about?
....
3 What is good in the film?
....
4 Do you want to watch it?
....

4 Think about a film you like. Answer the questions.

1 What is the name of the film? What kind of film is it?
....
2 Who do you watch the film with?
....
3 What is it about?
....
4 What characters are in the film?
....
5 What is good in the film?
....
6 Why do you think the film is great?
....

5 Write a film review. Use the paragraph guide from Exercise 3 and your notes from Exercise 4 to help you.

....
....
....
....
....
....

Past Lives

Vocabulary History

Brain Trainer

Draw a history word. It helps you remember it!

Now do Exercise 1.

★ **1** Look at the pictures. Complete the crossword.

Across

Down

★ **2** Choose the correct options.

1 The *dungeon* / *prisoner* was a cold and dark place.
2 The *army* / *castle* was big with strong walls.
3 Please don't *die* / *kill* that animal!
4 They don't clean the house or cook. They've got *servants* / *soldiers*.
5 King Edward III of England lived in the fourteenth *century* / *plague*.
6 When did the Second World *Sword* / *War* start?

★★ **3** Complete the sentences with these words.

castle	century	knight	plague
prisoner	servants	soldiers	war

1 A *century* is a hundred years.
2 There are thousands of .... in an army.
3 Their .... do all the jobs in the house.
4 The king put the .... in the dungeon.
5 The king and queen live in a ....
6 In a .... , thousands of people die.
7 The .... has got a big horse and a sword.
8 The .... is a terrible disease.

★★ **4** Complete the text with these words.

army	century	dying
killing	plague	queen

It is the fourteenth [1] *century*. The king and [2] .... are in the castle. The servants are bringing them food and drink. But outside, things are not good. There is a terrible war between the English and the French and the [3] .... of the English king is in France. Thousands of people are [4] .... in this war but there is also a [5] .... in Europe. This terrible disease is [6] .... rich and poor people.

Vocabulary page 106

Reading

★ **1** **Read the text quickly. Choose the best title.**
  a The Story of Merlin
  b The Story of King Arthur
  c The Story of Queen Guinevere

★ **2** **Read the text again. Choose the correct options.**
  1 Uther Pendragon / Sir Ector was Arthur's father.
  2 Uther Pendragon / Sir Ector looked after Arthur when he was a child.
  3 Arthur became king because he pulled a sword out of the ground / a stone.
  4 Arthur made a round table for Guinevere / his knights.
  5 Guinevere went to France with Lancelot / Arthur.
  6 Arthur died / didn't die in the war.

★★ **3** **Are the sentences true (T), false (F) or don't know (DK)?**
  1 Arthur's mother was Igraine of Cornwall.   T
  2 Sir Ector took Merlin away from his parents when he was a baby.   ....
  3 Arthur was eighteen years old when Uther died.   ....
  4 The table was round because there were many knights.   ....
  5 Arthur's knights all liked him.   ....
  6 The war started because Mordred tried to take the kingdom from Arthur.   ....

★★★ **4** **Complete the sentences.**
  1 Arthur's parents were Uther and Igraine.
  2 Uther died when Arthur was a .... man.
  3 The name of Arthur's .... was Camelot.
  4 Lancelot was the best .... in Camelot.
  5 Mordred started a .... and many knights died.

Arthur was the son of King Uther Pendragon and Igraine of Cornwall. When he was a baby, Merlin the magician took him away from his parents and he lived with a kind knight, Sir Ector. The years passed. Arthur became a young man and Uther died. There was no king in England.

Then, one day, a stone came out of the ground with a sword in it. Merlin said to the people, 'Pull the sword out of the stone and you can be king.' Many people tried, but only Arthur pulled out the sword. He became king!

Arthur built a castle called Camelot and he married Guinevere. Many knights came to Camelot and Arthur made a round table for them. The table was round to show that all the knights were equal. But they weren't really equal; the best knight was Sir Lancelot.

Lancelot and Queen Guinevere fell in love. They went to France and Arthur followed them. Arthur's son, Mordred, stayed in England. Arthur asked him to look after the country. But Mordred hated Arthur and he tried to take Arthur's country away from him. There was a war and most of the Knights of the Round Table died. But Arthur didn't die. Three queens took him to Avalon. Some people think Arthur is not dead now. They think he lives in Avalon today!

Grammar Past simple: affirmative and negative

★ 1 Choose the correct options.

Alice and Jake Williams ¹was / were at the castle yesterday. Their parents, Mr and Mrs Williams, ²wasn't / weren't with them. They ³was / were at home. The castle ⁴wasn't / weren't very big and it ⁵wasn't / weren't interesting. There ⁶was / were a dungeon but there ⁷wasn't / weren't prisoners in the dungeon. There ⁸was / were hundreds of people at the castle, but these people ⁹wasn't / weren't kings, queens or knights. It ¹⁰was / were boring!

★ 2 Complete the sentences with the Past simple form of these verbs .

come	do	give	have	meet
not stay	not visit	~~read~~	send	take

1 I *read* the book last year in school.
2 We .... dinner an hour ago.
3 Karen .... me an email yesterday.
4 Oscar and Matt .... to my house yesterday.
5 He .... in a hotel.
6 They .... their friends outside the cinema.
7 Mum .... the dog for a walk in the park.
8 She .... her little brother a toy sword for his birthday.
9 They .... the museum.
10 They .... their homework and went to bed.

★★ 3 Complete the email with the Past simple form of the verbs.

New Message   Send

Hi Ben

How are you? I ¹*had* (have) a great weekend. On Saturday I ²........................ (go) mountain biking with friends. We ³........................ (visit) an old castle in the countryside. It ⁴........................ (be) interesting, but we ⁵........................ (not see) any ghosts! In the afternoon, my friend Emma ⁶........................ (come) to my house. We ⁷........................ (watch) a new DVD about monsters. Emma ⁸........................ (not like) it because she hates scary films!

Speak soon,
Samantha

★★ 4 Complete the story with the Past simple form of these verbs.

eat	feel	~~go~~	have	not go
not listen	say	stay	watch	

Last night Ursula's parents ¹*went* to the cinema. Ursula ²........................ with them. She ³........................ at home. 'Be good and go to sleep early,' her mother ⁴........................ .
But Ursula ⁵........................ to her mother. She ⁶........................ a horror film on TV. At midnight she ⁷........................ hungry, so she ⁸........................ pizza and ice cream. That night she ⁹........................ a bad dream.

3

Grammar Reference pages 90–91

Vocabulary Life events

★ 1 Match these words to the pictures.

die	fall in love	graduate
have a baby	retire	~~start school~~

start school

....

....

....

★ 2 Choose the correct options.

1 *move / leave* house
2 *have / be* born
3 *go / get* married
4 *go / have* to university
5 *leave / have* home
6 *be / find* a job
7 *leave / get* school

★ 3 Match the beginnings (1–5) to the endings (a–e).

1 Maria and Manuel got   *d*
2 Natasha and Ivan had
3 Maurice fell in
4 Grandpa left
5 I found

a a baby last month.
b a job in a clothes shop.
c love with Claudette.
d married last year.
e school when he was seventeen.

★★ 4 Complete the sentences with the Past simple form of these verbs.

be born	~~get married~~	graduate
move house	retire	start school

1 My parents fell in love when they were at university and *got married* five years later.
2 Alexander .... with top marks from a very good university.
3 Beth .... six months ago, but she still can't read!
4 Mr Evans .... when he was sixty-six years old. Now he stays at home and works in his garden.
5 I .... on 4th July 2000.
6 We lived in the centre of town for many years, but we .... a year ago.

★★ 5 Complete the text with the Past simple form of these verbs.

~~be born~~	be born	fall in love
find a job	get married	leave home
leave school	retire	start school

Mark Jones [1] *was born* in 1915 and he
[2] .... when he was six. Mark didn't like studying and he [3] .... ten years later. He [4] .... in a shop in town. One day, a pretty girl called Ivy Brown came into the shop to buy something. Mark [5] .... with her and they [6] .... in 1937. Their first baby, Eliza, [7] .... two years later. Mark, Ivy and Eliza were very happy together. The years passed. Eliza grew up and [8] .... Mark and Ivy became grandparents. Mark [9] .... when he was seventy. He died fifteen years later and Ivy died a month after Mark.

Vocabulary page 106

Reasoning

Speaking and Listening

★ 1 🔊 1.8 **Complete the conversations with these words. Then listen and check.**

because	because	not
silly	~~why~~	why

1 A *Why* do you want to go to the park?
  B .... we can go skateboarding there.

2 A Let's go to the park this afternoon.
  B Don't be ....! It's snowing.

3 A I don't want to go for a walk.
  B Why .... ? It's a nice day. Come on!

4 A I want to go to the library.
  B .... ?
  A .... it's got some great history books.

★ 2 **Match the questions and statements (1–4) to the responses (a–d).**

1 I don't want to go to university. *c*
2 Why don't you want to go to the zoo?
3 I hated the dungeon.
4 Why do you want to visit the castle?

a Because it's really cool!
b Because it's boring!
c Why not?
d Why?

★★ 3 🔊 1.9 **Complete the conversation with these phrases. Then listen and check.**

because	because	because	don't be
why	~~why don't you~~	why not	

Carlos Let's go to the park this afternoon.
Nadia No, thanks.
Carlos Oh, come on, Nadia! [1] *Why don't you* want to come?
Nadia [2] .... it's cold.
Carlos Then let's watch a DVD at my house.
Jody Not again, Carlos!
Carlos [3] .... ?
Jody [4] .... we always watch DVDs at your house, or my house, or Nadia's house. Let's visit the castle.
Zak [5] .... ?
Jody Well, [6] .... it's fun. And there are dungeons …
Carlos Jody's right. The castle's got a great shop. I bought some cool things from there last year.
Nadia What did you buy?
Carlos A DVD. In the evening we can watch the DVD.
Nadia Carlos! [7] _____ silly!

★★ 4 **Read the conversation in Exercise 3 again. Are the sentences true (T), false (F) or don't know (DK)?**

1 Nadia doesn't want to go to the park.   *T*
2 The friends always watch DVDs at Carlos's house.   ....
3 Jody went to the castle last year.   ....
4 The friends often visit the castle.   ....
5 The shop at the castle sells DVDs.   ....
6 Zak wants to watch a DVD in the evening.   ....

★★★ 5 **Complete the conversation between Tom and Zoe. Use the information in the table and expressions from Exercises 1 and 2.**

Friday	go out ✘, stay at home ✓, study for a test on Monday	
Saturday	get up early ✓, help mum in the shop	
Sunday	go to the cinema ✘, saw a film last week	

Tom Let's go out on Friday.
Zoe I don't want to go out on Friday.
Tom Why not?
Zoe …

Grammar Past simple: questions and short answers

★ 1 Match the questions (1–6) to the answers (a–f).

1 Did you visit the castle last week?   c
2 Did Dave see the prisoner in the dungeon?
3 Did the friends watch a historical film last night?
4 Did Anna enjoy the party?
5 Did the First World War start in 1914?
6 Did you and your friends go home by bus?

a Yes, he did.
b No, we didn't.
c No, I didn't.
d Yes, it did.
e No, she didn't.
f Yes, they did.

★ 2 Complete the questions.

1 Mum left the house early this morning.
Did dad leave (dad / leave) early, too?

2 I read the book.
.... (she / read) it, too?

3 I wrote the email.
.... (you / write) the text message, too?

4 I heard a noise outside.
.... (he / hear) it, too?

5 The fire burned all the houses.
.... (it / burn) the castle, too?

6 He gave her a present.
.... (they / give) her a present, too?

Brain Trainer

Writing questions? Remember these four steps:

1 A = Auxiliary | Did
2 S = Subject | she
3 I = Infinitive | play tennis
4 T = Time | yesterday?

Now do Exercise 3.

★★ 3 Complete the conversation.

Sophie Hi, Thomas. [1] *Did you visit the castle today?* (you / visit / the castle / today?)

Thomas Yes, I [2] .... I went with Amy. She loves old buildings.

Sophie [3] ....
(you / see / the dungeons?)

Thomas Yes, we [4] ....

Sophie [5] ....
(Amy / like / them?)

Thomas No, she [6] .... There were spiders and she's scared of spiders.

Sophie [7] ....
(you and Amy / see / rats in the dungeons?)

Thomas No, we [8] .... The dungeons don't have rats!

★★★ 4 Write the questions for the answers.

1 A *When did Julia and Brian get married?*
  B Julia and Brian got married three years ago.

2 A .... ?
  B The fire started in the kitchen.

3 A .... ?
  B She wrote a wonderful book about King Arthur.

4 A .... ?
  B My brother graduated from university last year.

5 A .... ?
  B We met Alison in the park.

6 A .... ?
  B I went to the museum because I wanted to see the swords.

Grammar Reference pages 90–91

Reading

1 Read the page from the book quickly. Find:

1 six dates   *1485,* ....
2 two countries   ....
3 six languages   ....
....
4 two English names for boys
....
5 two sports   ....

From Princess of Spain to Queen of England

Katherine of Aragon was born near Madrid in Spain in 1485. Her parents were King Ferdinand and Queen Isabella. Katherine was beautiful and she was also very clever. She spoke and wrote in Latin and Spanish and she also spoke English, Flemish, French and Greek. She studied many subjects, including mathematics and philosophy, and she enjoyed dancing, music, archery and horse-riding.

In 1501 Katherine got married to Prince Arthur of England, but Arthur died five months later. It was a very difficult time for Katherine. Then, in 1509 Katherine got married to Arthur's brother, Henry. She was twenty-three and Henry was seventeen. Two weeks after their wedding, Henry and Katherine became King and Queen of England.

At first they were happy and the English people loved Katherine. But Henry wanted a son and unfortunately, he and Katherine had only one daughter, Mary. In 1525, Henry fell in love with Anne Boleyn and he wanted to get married again. He divorced Katherine and, in 1533, he got married to Anne Boleyn.

Katherine left the castle. Her life was sad and lonely. On 7th January, 1536, she died at Kimbolton Castle. Her daughter Mary became Queen of England when Henry died.

❀ 2 ❀

2 Read the page again. Put the information in the correct order.

a Katherine and Henry got married.   ....
b Katherine and Henry became King and Queen of England.   ....
c Katherine was born near Madrid.   *1*
d Anne Boleyn and Henry got married.   ....
e Henry divorced Katherine.   ....
f Katherine's husband, Arthur, died.   ....
g Katherine and Henry's daughter was born.   ....

3 Match the sentence beginnings (1–7) to the endings (a–g).

1 Katherine's parents were   *d*
2 Katherine enjoyed
3 Arthur was
4 In 1509 Katherine and Henry
5 Katherine and Henry's daughter
6 Henry fell in love with
7 Mary became Queen of England

a got married.
b Anne Boleyn.
c was Mary.
d King Ferdinand and Queen Isabella.
e when her father died.
f Henry's brother.
g dancing and music.

Listening

1 🔊 1.10 Listen to Kate and Nick talking about a film. Tick the things they mention.

castle ☐
clothes ☐
food ☐
money ☐
rats ☐
shoes ☐

2 🔊 1.10 Listen again. Choose the correct options.

1 Nick *loved* / *didn't mind* the film *Marie Antoinette*.
2 Kate wants to watch it because she likes the *clothes* / *music* in the film.
3 Marie Antoinette *was* / *wasn't* French.
4 She got married when she was *fifteen* / *nineteen*.
5 She became Queen of France when she was *fifteen* / *nineteen*.
6 Kate learned about Marie Antoinette from a *documentary* / *book*.

Writing A biography

1 Read the text. In what order is the information in a biography?

1 Other information ....
2 Work ....
3 Name, place and date of birth .A.
4 Education ....

Patrick Walker

(A) My granddad's name is Patrick Walker. He was born in Ireland in 1945. There were seven boys in the family!

(B) My granddad didn't like school and he didn't want to go to university. He left school when he was sixteen.

(C) He found a job in a shoe shop. He also worked in a cinema at the weekend. He didn't mind because he loved watching the films.

(D) In 1963 Granddad moved from Ireland to New York. It was exciting because there were lots of things to do there. Granddad loved listening to music in cafés. One day a beautiful woman called Rita sang in the café and Granddad fell in love with her. In 1965 they got married and they had one son – my dad!

2 Complete the table with the information about Patrick Walker.

Name	¹ *Patrick Walker*
Place of birth	2 ....
Date of birth	3 ....
Education	4 ....
Work	5 .... 6 ....
Other information	7 .... 8 .... 9 .... 10 ....

3 Read the biography again. Answer the questions.

1 Where and when was Patrick born?
He was born in Ireland in 1945.

2 How many brothers did he have?
....

3 Did he go to university?
....

4 When did he leave school?
....

5 What job did he find?
....

6 What did he do at the weekend?
....

7 Did he mind working at the weekend?
....

8 What happened in 1963?
....

9 Who did he meet in a café in New York?
....

10 When did he get married?
....

4 Think of a person in your family. Write information about him/her in the table.

Name	....
Place of birth	....
Date of birth	....
Education	....
Work	....
Other information	....

5 Write a biography about a person in your family. Use the paragraph guide from Exercise 1 and your notes from Exercise 4 to help you.

....
....
....
....
....

Grammar

1 Choose the correct options.

New Message   ⊗

Send

Hi Emilie,

I ⁰ *'m writing* this email to you from a great hotel.
Mum and I are in New York! We ¹.... here every
summer because Mum's an actress. She doesn't
².... in films. She ³.... ⁴.... in the theatre. At the
moment, she ⁵.... the words of a new play. She
often ⁶.... me to help her. I ⁷.... mind ⁸.... it
because I ⁹.... to be an actress one day, too.
What about you? What ¹⁰.... to be?

Love,
Jacqueline

0	**a** write	**b** writes	**c** 'm writing
1	**a** come	**b** coming	**c** comes
2	**a** act	**b** acts	**c** acting
3	**a** love	**b** loves	**c** loving
4	**a** work	**b** works	**c** working
5	**a** learning	**b** 's learning	**c** learns
6	**a** is asking	**b** asking	**c** asks
7	**a** 'm not	**b** not	**c** don't
8	**a** do	**b** doing	**c** does
9	**a** want	**b** wanting	**c** wants

10 a you want
    b do you want
    c does you want

/ 10 marks

**2 Complete the sentences with the Past simple
form of the verbs.**

0 Emily's friends went to the castle yesterday,
but Emily *didn't go* (not go).

1 Andrea and Max .... (not be) at
my house last night.

2 .... (you / stop) at the café
after school?

3 They .... (leave) the party
at 11 p.m.

4 She .... (carry) her laptop to
school in her bag.

5 I .... (see) a great film on TV
last night.

6 .... (your mum / make) breakfast
for you this morning?

7 We .... (have) an interesting
History lesson yesterday.

8 Harry .... (not do) all his
homework last night.

9 The young athlete .... (take) part
in the Olympic Games.

10 When .... (the King of France /
die)?

/ 10 marks

Vocabulary

3 Choose the correct options.

0 Did you watch the (documentary) / western / fantasy about dolphins on TV? It was interesting and I learned a lot.

1 I didn't like the action film. I thought it was *expensive / rubbish / tasty*.

2 Romeo and Juliet *got / fell / went* in love and wanted to get married.

3 I went ice-skating with my friends at the ice-skating *belt / court / rink*.

4 The boys aren't here. They're playing football on the football *court / pitch / pool*.

5 When did he *move / graduate / retire* house?

6 We practise every day at the *athletics / basketball / archery* track.

7 I didn't understand the science fiction film. The story was *romantic / sad / weird*.

8 The famous artist lived in the fifteenth *century / plague / war*.

9 The *queen / knight / servant* worked in the kitchen of the castle.

10 What did the student do when he *had / graduated / be* from university?

/ 10 marks

Speaking

4 Complete the conversation with these words.

about	because	boring	favourite
~~go~~	great	idea	in
thanks	that's	why	

Jane Let's ⁰*go* to the cinema tonight.
Rob ¹........................ a good idea. There's a fantastic war film on.
Will I'm ²........................ . I love war films. They're my ³........................ type of film.
Lucy No, ⁴........................ . I don't want to go to the cinema.
Jane ⁵........................ don't you want to go?
Lucy ⁶........................ I think war films are ⁷........................ .
Rob Well, what ⁸........................ a horror film?
Will That's a good ⁹........................ . I've got a great DVD about ghosts.
Jane ¹⁰........................ !

/ 10 marks

Translation

5 Translate the sentences.

1 I enjoy going swimming in the summer.
2 We don't usually play basketball on this basketball court.
3 My brother is annoying.
4 The prisoner is in the dungeon.
5 The plague killed thousands of people.

/ 5 marks

Dictation

6))) 1.11 Listen and write.

/ 5 marks

4 Is It A Crime?

Vocabulary Breaking the rules

⭐ **1** Look at the pictures. Complete the labels.

bully	~~cheat~~	drop	fight
lie	play	spray	steal

cheat in an exam

.... over a T-shirt

.... to your parents

.... a younger student

.... graffiti

.... a purse

.... litter

.... loud music

Brain Trainer

Find words that go together:

drop *litter*   spray *graffiti*

Now do Exercise 2.

⭐ **2** Match 1–6 to a–f to make phrases.

1 copy   a graffiti
2 spray   b litter
3 drop   c truant
4 use   d a friends' homework
5 play   e rude
6 be   f a mobile phone in class

⭐⭐ **3** Complete the sentences with verbs from Exercise 1.

1 She *lies* to her parents but they never believe her.
2 I can't hear you. Why do you .... loud music all the time?
3 The boys .... at school when they are angry.
4 I never .... litter because it is bad for the environment.
5 Melissa and her friends .... graffiti in the park. They think it's exciting.
6 The older students sometimes .... the younger ones and take their money and food.

⭐⭐ **4** Complete the text with these words.

bully	copy	exams	fight
~~rude~~	truant	use	

The students in Mrs Braddock's class are never [1] *rude*. They always say 'please' and 'thank you'. They always come to lessons and never play [2] .... The boys don't [3] .... and the bigger students don't [4] .... the smaller ones and take their money. They never [5] .... their mobile phones in class and they never, ever cheat in [6] .... or [7] .... their friend's homework. They're scared of Mrs Braddock!

Vocabulary page 107

Reading

★ 1 **Read the story summary quickly. Choose the correct options.**

1 Kevin Smith's students *broke / didn't break* the school rules.

2 There was a dance competition *at school / on TV.*

★ 2 **Read the story summary again. Match the sentence beginnings (1–5) to the endings (a–e).**

1 When Kevin met his new students,   *c*

2 On Kevin's first day at Morton High School,

3 The students liked

4 The dance classes

5 On the day of the competition

a the students were excited.

b were fun for the students.

c they were breaking the rules.

d he was angry.

e music and sport.

★★ 3 **What school rules were students breaking on Kevin's first day at school?**

1 *Max was doing his homework in class.*

2 *Nicola* ....

3 ....

4 ....

5 ....

★★★ 4 **Answer the questions.**

1 What was Kevin's job?
He was a music teacher.

2 What did he think of Amy's graffiti?
....

3 Where were Derek and Miles?
....

4 What was Carla doing?
....

5 How did Kevin get his idea about the dance classes?
....

6 How did the students feel about the dance classes?
....

Story summary: **From Good to Bad?**

It was the first day at Morton High School for music teacher, Kevin Smith, but when he met his students, he wasn't happy. Max was doing his English homework in class and Nicola was copying it. And Amy was spraying graffiti on the wall! Yes, it was a good picture and the colours were beautiful, but she was still breaking the rules. Derek and Miles were fighting at the back of the classroom, Carla was eating sweets and dropping her litter on the floor. Kevin was angry. He had a very difficult job to do.

One day, Kevin was on the school football pitch. The students were talking and he was listening to them. Kevin learned something important about these young people – they liked sport and they loved music. Suddenly, he had an idea. Every year there was a dance competition on TV and Kevin wanted his students to enter the competition. He started dance classes and the students came to them. At first, the classes were difficult for the students. But the students enjoyed the classes – and they also started to enjoy their other lessons. They didn't break the rules, they listened to their teachers and they passed their exams.

The day of the dance competition came. The students were excited. They were on TV and their friends were watching them! Did they win the competition? Buy the book and find out!

Grammar Past continuous

★ **1** Look at the picture. Put the words in order to make sentences.

1 sitting / Two young women / were / in the police station
Two young women were sitting in the police station.

2 wasn't / The police officer / talking / to them
....

3 the two young women / doing / were / What / ?
....

4 and his dog / weren't / The old man / sitting / on chairs
....

5 leaving / was / the police station / An old woman
....

6 wasn't / a drink / The boy / stealing
....

7 Was / wearing / a football shirt / the boy / ?
....

★ **2** Complete the questions in the Past simple. Then look at the picture and answer them.

1 A *Were* the two young women sitting on chairs?
B *Yes, they were.*

2 A .... the police officer talking to them?
B ....

3 A .... the old man and his dog eating?
B ....

4 A .... the boy wearing football boots?
B ....

5 A .... the little girl sleeping?
B ....

6 A .... the man and the woman talking to the police officer?
B ....
....

★★ **3** Complete the sentences with the Past continuous form of the verbs.

1 The police officer *was standing* (stand) behind a desk.

2 There was a man in front of the desk, but he ....
(not talk) to the police officer.

3 'What .... the little girl .... (do)?' 'She .... (steal) a watch.'

4 The two young women .... (listen) to music.

5 The old man and his dog .... (sleep).

6 The old woman .... (not carry) a box. She .... (carry) a big bag.

7 What .... the man and the woman .... (fight) about?

★★ **4** What were you and your family doing at eight o'clock last night? You can use these ideas or your own ideas. Write five sentences.

cook dinner	do homework
read the newspaper	talk to a friend
watch TV	write emails

Vocabulary Prepositions of movement

★ **1** Look at the pictures. Complete the crossword.

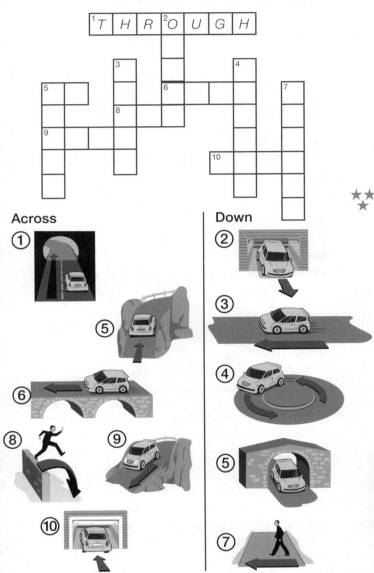

| ¹T | H | R | ²O | U | G | H |

Across

①
⑤
⑥
⑧
⑨
⑩

Down

②
③
④
⑤
⑦

★ **2** Choose the correct options.

1 Walk *across* / *out of* the street to the other side.
2 We walked *through* / *along* the beach.
3 Dora went *out of* / *into* her bedroom and sat on her bed.
4 The mouse ran *under* / *through* the table.
5 The teacher was walking *over* / *around* the classroom.
6 Dad came *out of* / *down* the house.
7 The aeroplane flew *over* / *off* the town.
8 Come *up* / *down* from that tree! It's time for dinner!

★★ **3** Complete the text with these words.

| along | into | off | out of | over | ~~through~~ | up |

1 Martin looked *through* the window.
2 Sarah climbed .... a mountain. It was very tiring.
3 The mouse walked .... the wall.
4 Harry jumped .... the bridge .... the water.
5 Sophie walked .... the bridge.
6 I took the present .... the box.

★★★ **4** Complete the text with these words.

| across | along | down | into |
| into | through | ~~up~~ | |

Will Adams climbed ¹*up* the ladder. Then he climbed ² .... the bedroom ³ .... an open window. A police officer was walking ⁴ .... the street. She saw Will and ran ⁵ .... the road to the house. At that moment, Will came ⁶ .... the ladder again. 'Good evening, Officer,' he said. 'My key was in the bedroom. Now I've got it and I can go ⁷ .... the house and make some tea. Would you like a cup?'

Vocabulary page 107

 **Chatroom** Showing interest

Speaking and Listening

Brain Trainer

Do you want to show surprise? Say: *Really?*

Good news? Say: *That's great!* or *That's amazing!*

Bad news? Say: *Oh no!* or *Poor you.*

Now do Exercise 1.

★ **1** **1.12 Choose the correct options. Then listen and check.**

1 A Mum burned her hand while she was cooking.
  B *That's amazing! /* (*Oh no!*)

2 A I won £10,000 in a competition last year!
  B *That's great! / At last!*

3 A I saw the Queen of England yesterday!
  B *Really? / Oh no?* Where did you see her?

4 A At last! You're late! What happened?
  B *Poor you. / You'll never guess!*

5 A I lost my bag on the bus yesterday.
  B *That's great! / Poor you.*

★ **2** **Put the conversation in the correct order.**

a Well, what happened? ....
b Really? ....
c I saw Sean Paul in town a few minutes ago. ....
d At last! Where were you? *1.*
e That's amazing! ....
f Yes, he was shopping and I spoke to him. ....
g You'll never guess! ....

Speaking and Listening page 116

★★ **3** **1.13 Complete the conversation with these phrases. Then listen and check.**

| ~~at~~ | guess | happened | poor | really | that's |

Nadia Jody! ¹*At* last! Why are you late?
Jody Sorry. I missed the bus and walked here.
Nadia Oh no! ² .... you! What happened?
Jody You'll never ³ .... ! I saw Alicia Keys in the town centre!
Nadia ⁴ .... ? I don't believe you!
Jody It's true! There was a man behind her and he was stealing money from her bag.
Nadia What did you do?
Jody I shouted and he ran away.
Nadia Then what ⁵ .... ?
Jody Alicia heard me. She thanked me and she gave me two tickets to her concert on Saturday.
Nadia ⁶ .... amazing! What are you going to do with them?
Jody I'm going to go to the concert – with you!
Nadia Thanks, Jody! You're a great friend!

★★ **4** **Read the conversation in Exercise 3 again. Answer the questions.**

1 Why was Jody late?
  She was late because she missed the bus.

2 Where did she see Alicia Keys?
  ....

3 How did Nadia feel when Jody told her about Alicia?
  ....

4 What was the man doing?
  ....

5 How did Alicia thank Jody?
  ....

6 When is Alicia's concert?
  ....

★★ **5** **Imagine one of your friends has good news and another friend has bad news. Write two conversations and show interest. You can use your own ideas or the ideas below.**

| **Friend 1** | win a prize / meet a famous athlete |
| **Friend 2** | lose money / break computer |

Grammar Past simple and Past continuous

★ **1** Read the sentences. Write PS (Past simple) or PC (Past continuous).

1 They were watching TV.   .PC.
2 Julia saw us.   ....
3 We were sitting in the café.   ....
4 She was writing an email.   ....
5 The phone rang.   ....
6 They heard a noise.   ....

★ **2** Use two sentences from Exercise 1 to make a sentence with *when*. Then rewrite the sentence with *while*.

1 *(1+6) They were watching TV when they heard a noise.*
2 *(1+6) While they were watching TV, they heard a noise.*
3 ....
4 ....
5 ....
6 ....

★★ **3** Choose the correct options.

1 While we *walked / were walking* home, it *started / was starting* to rain.
2 I *had / was having* a shower when the lights *went out / were going out*.
3 When Mum *came / were coming* home, Dad *made / was making* dinner in the kitchen.
4 Mrs Jones *slept / was sleeping* when the thieves *climbed / were climbing* through the living room window.
5 I *found / was finding* this interesting website while I *looked / was looking* for information on the Internet.
6 The teacher *came / was coming* into the classroom while the students *wrote / were writing* on the board.

★★ **4** Complete the sentences with the Past simple and Past continuous forms of the verbs.

1 While the thief *was climbing* (climb) up the ladder, the police .... (arrive).

2 When the teacher .... (walk) into the classroom, the boys .... (fight).

3 .... you .... (play) loud music when I .... (phone) you?

4 While Sam .... (ride) his bike in the park, he .... (lose) his mobile.

★★★ **5** Write sentences with the Past simple and Past continuous forms of the verbs.

1 while / Sam / run / he / drop / his money
While Sam was running, he dropped his money.
2 when / we / see / the thief / he / climb / through the window
....
3 they / travel / around the world / when / they / lose / their bags
....
4 my little brother / run / into the kitchen / while / I / make / dinner
....
5 they / sleep / when / the fire / start
....
6 what / you / do / when / I / phone?
....

Grammar Reference pages 92–93

Reading

1 **Read the email quickly. What is the email about?**

a Maria's birthday presents
b Maria and her friends
c Maria, the bicycle thief and a Smartphone

New Message ⊗

Hi Luke,

Send

Thank you for remembering my birthday yesterday. Yes, I got some great presents: Mum and Dad gave me a BMX bike and Gran gave me a Smartphone! And yes, I had a great day. In fact, it was very exciting. Let me tell you about it.

In the morning I went to the park on my BMX. There I met Emily and Roger and we played basketball for an hour. Then we sat under a tree to eat our sandwiches. I was showing them my new Smartphone when I noticed that my BMX bike was missing! I jumped up and looked around the park. And then I saw it! A boy with a black jacket was stealing my bike. 'Stop!' I shouted, but the boy got on the bike and rode over the bridge. Then I remembered my Smartphone, so I took a photo of him and called the police.

When the police officer arrived, we showed him the photo of the boy. 'Come with me to the police station,' he said. We were following the police officer over the bridge when we heard a noise. We looked over the side and what do you think we saw? It was the boy in the photo! He was sitting on the grass. 'Please help me', he said, 'I fell off the bike and I broke my leg.'

Well, I got my bike back. It was lucky I had my new Smartphone with me.

See you soon!
Maria

---

2 **Read the email again. Answer the questions.**

1 Who gave Maria a Smartphone?
Her grandmother gave her a Smartphone.

2 Where did Maria meet her friends?
....

3 When did Maria notice her bike was missing?
....

4 What was the thief wearing?
....

5 What did the thief do when Maria shouted?
....

6 What happened to the thief?
....

3 **Choose the correct options.**

1 Luke asked Maria about her *bike /* (*birthday*).
2 Maria met her friends at the *park / sports centre*.
3 The friends *were / weren't* playing basketball when a boy stole Maria's bike.
4 The thief *was / wasn't* riding the bike when Maria saw him.
5 Maria took a photo of *the thief / her friends*.
6 The thief was on *the bridge / the grass* when the police officer saw him.

Listening

1 🔊 **1.14** **Listen to four conversations. Match the conversations 1–4 to the pictures a–d.**

2 🔊 **1.14** **Listen again. Match the sentence beginnings (1–6) to the endings (a–f).**

1 Anna
2 Max
3 Eva
4 Sam
5 Lisa
6 Dave

a didn't listen to his brother.
b was cheating.
c had her name in the book.
d was dropping litter.
e was stealing.
f thought the music was loud.

Writing A short story

1 Read the short text. Find four sequencing words.

Last Saturday I went out with my friends. First, we played football. Next we had an ice cream. Then we went swimming. Finally, we went to the cinema and watched a film.

1 *First*   **3** ....

2 ....   **4** ....

2 Read the story. Put the pictures (a–d) in the correct order.

It was nine o'clock in the morning when Sam and his friends arrived at the school. There was a lot of litter in the schoolyard and it was ugly and dirty.

First, they put the litter in the bin. Next, they looked at the walls of the school. Then they sprayed graffiti on the walls. The graffiti was fantastic! Finally, they washed their hands and had some sandwiches.

A man was walking along the street when he saw Sam and his friends. He was angry and he shouted at them. But Sam showed the man a poster. It said: 'Graffiti Competition this Saturday'. 'It's OK,' said Sam. 'We weren't breaking the rules! We were making the school beautiful.'

3 Read the story again. Answer the questions.

1 What time was it when Sam and his friends arrived at the school?
It was nine o'clock in the morning.

2 What did the friends do with the litter?
....

3 What did they do to the walls of the school?
....

4 Why was the man angry?
....

5 What did Sam show the man?
....

4 Write a story. Use the words and pictures to help you.

last weekend / sunny / snowboarding
first: go up the mountain
next: snowboard down the mountain
then: go to a café / have a drink / a man steal their snowboards / stand up to leave / snowboards were missing
finally: call police / police arrive with snowboards / say: 'It was easy / find thief. We just / follow / across the snow.'

Last weekend it was sunny. Naomi and Liam went snowboarding …

5 Look At You

Vocabulary Appearance adjectives

★ **1** Choose the correct options.

① He's *short* / *tall*.

② He's got a *big beard* / *moustache*.

③ Her hair is *curly* / *straight*.

④ She's got a *short* / *long* black hair.

⑤ He's got a *beard* / *moustache*.

⑥ They're *slim* / *well-built*.

⑦ They've got short *fair* / *dark* hair.

⑧ She's got *glasses* / *a beard*.

★ **2** Complete the sentences with these words.

dark	~~short~~	slim	straight	tall

1 Paul's hair isn't *short*. It's long.
2 Andrea and Luis haven't got .... hair. They've got fair hair.
3 Veronica doesn't like her .... hair. She wants curly hair.
4 Emma is .... but her brother is well-built.
5 I'm not short. I'm ....

★★ **3** Write questions and answers.

1 George / be / slim? ✘
   Is George slim? No, he isn't.
2 George / be / short? ✔
   ....
3 Rachel / be / short? ✘
   ....
4 Rachel / have got / fair hair? ✔
   ....
5 George / have got / straight hair? ✘
   ....

★★★ **4** Look at the photo. Complete the description with these words.

dark	fair	glasses	long
moustache	slim	~~straight~~	

I think John and Vanessa are great. John's got short [1] *straight* [2] .... hair but Vanessa's got [3] .... curly [4] .... hair. They're not very tall, but they're both [5] .... because they do a lot of exercise. John's got a beard and a [6] .... He sometimes wears [7] .... , but he isn't wearing them in this picture.

Vocabulary page 108

Reading

★ **1** Read the letters quickly. Match the questions (1–2) to the letters (A–B).

1 Are my friends right?

2 Why does she say 'no'?

Brain Trainer

Underline the adjectives in the letters.

interesting, long, dark

Now do Exercise 2.

★ **2** Read the letters again. Choose the correct options.

1 Laura's got long, *fair /* (*brown*) hair.

2 Laura thinks her hair is *boring / interesting*.

3 Maddy thinks Laura's mum is *wrong / right*.

4 Charlie's friends think he's *silly / great*.

5 Charlie's a *good / bad* basketball player.

★★ **3** Match the people in the letters to the sentences.

1 These people are tall. *Julia* and *Ed*

2 This person is well-built. ....

3 This person has got brown eyes.

....

4 This person has got green eyes.

....

5 This person has got brown hair.

....

6 This person has got dark hair. ....

7 These people have got long hair.

.... and ....

8 This person has got very short hair.

....

★★ **4** Answer the questions.

1 What colour was Laura's hair when she was young? *It was fair.*

2 Who doesn't want Laura to change the colour of her hair? ....

3 What colour eyes has Laura got?

....

4 What sport does Charlie play?

....

5 Who are Sam and Ed? ....

Write to Maddy – she's here to help!

(A) Dear Maddy

Please help me. All my friends look interesting. Julia's got long dark hair and green eyes and she's very tall. Mary's got really short red hair and she looks great! I've got long, brown hair and I hate it. It's boring. When I was young, I had beautiful fair hair. Now I want to change my hair colour and have shorter hair but my mum says 'No way!' Is she right? Fair hair, red hair or dark hair is more beautiful than brown hair.
Laura

Hi Laura

Your mum's right. You look fantastic in the photo. Brown hair is better for you because you've got beautiful brown eyes. Why don't you change your hairstyle? It's easier to change the style than the colour.
Maddy

(B) Dear Maddy

I'm the shortest person in my class and I hate it. My friend Sam isn't tall, but he's taller than me, and my friend Ed is the tallest person in the class. He's also well-built. When we play basketball, I look silly. Ed says, 'You don't look silly. You're the fastest player in the team.' I'm a good basketball player but I want to be tall. What can I do?
Charlie

Hi Charlie

We sometimes want to change our appearance but we can't always do it. Ed's right. You don't look silly and your friends think you're great. You're a good basketball player, you're faster than the other players and your friends love having you in the team!
Maddy

Grammar

Comparatives and Superlatives

★ **1** Complete the table with the correct form of these adjectives.

bad	beautiful	~~big~~	curly
exciting	expensive	good	slim
special	strange	tasty	young

Short adjectives	Comparative	Superlative
big	*bigger*	*the biggest*

Long adjectives	Comparative	Superlative

Irregular adjectives	Comparative	Superlative

2 Choose the correct options.

1 Sylvia is *cleverer* / *the cleverest* girl in our class.
2 A horse is *bigger* / *the biggest* than a dog.
3 This is *more expensive* / *the most expensive* hotel in town.
4 His bike is *better* / *the best* than mine.
5 Which is *more boring* / *the most boring* subject at school?
6 Which was *funnier* / *the funniest* film?
7 Brad Pitt is *more famous* / *the most famous* than him.
8 You're *more wonderful* / *the most wonderful* dad in the world!

Grammar Reference pages 94–95

★★ **3** Complete the sentences with the comparative form of the adjectives.

1 Andrea's got *longer* (long) hair than her sister.
2 Paris is a .... (romantic) city than London.
3 Jack's book is good, but Adam's book is .... (exciting).
4 Jenny is .... (slim) and .... (tall) than Max.

★★ **4** Write sentences with superlative adjectives.

1 the Bugatti Veyron / be / expensive / car / in the shop
   The Bugatti Veyron is the most expensive car in the shop.

2 this film / have got / good / special effects
   ....

3 I think / funny / programme on TV / be / *The Simpsons*
   ....

4 the blue diamond / be / expensive / jewel / in the shop
   ....

5 London / be / big / city / in Britain
   ....

★★★ **5** Read the information. Then write sentences to compare Mike, Alice and Katie.

Name: Mike Stevenson
Age: 16
Appearance: 1.70 m, short dark hair, brown eyes
Hobbies: athletics and snowboarding

Name: Alice Norton
Age: 15
Appearance: 1.54 m, fair hair, blue eyes
Hobbies: books and films

Name: Katie Harris
Age: 17
Appearance: 1.62 m long dark hair, brown eyes
Hobbies: dancing and judo

1 old   *Mike is older than Alice but Katie is the oldest.*
2 short   ....
3 tall   ....
4 curly hair   ....
5 exciting hobbies   ....

Vocabulary

Personality adjectives

★ **1** Put the letters in the correct order to make personality adjectives. Use the letters in the grey squares to make an extra word.

1 DYFNEILR — F R I E N D L Y
2 SRENGEOU
3 DYOMO
4 LESFIHS
5 HYS
6 ITETLAAKV
7 RLECVE
8 NELNYDIUFR

★ **2** Look at the pictures. Complete the sentences.

Daisy is *shy* with new friends.

Jane is h _ _ _ -w _ _ _ _ _ _ .
She does a lot of things every day.

Mr Pea is s _ _ _ _ _ .
He can't do the test.

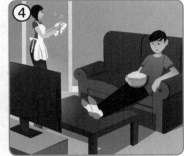

Bruce is l _ _ _ . He never helps his mum.

atrice is very c _ _ _ _ _ .
She is good at Maths.

Bryan and Jessica are c _ _ _ _ _ _ _ today.

★★ **3** Complete the text with the opposite adjectives.

Polly and Ella are twins, but their personalities are very different. In fact, Polly is the opposite of Ella!

Polly is hard-working, but Ella is [1] *lazy*.

Polly is always cheerful, but Ella is [2] ....

Polly is clever, but Ella is [3] ....

Polly is very generous, but Ella is often [4] ....

Polly is friendly, but Ella doesn't like people and she is [5] ....

Polly is talkative, but Ella is [6] ....

★★★ **4** Complete the text with the correct personality adjectives.

I enjoy being with people and am very [1] *friendly*. That's why I've got lots of friends! I'm not [2] s......................... and I love meeting new people. I don't like it when people are [3] u......................... and don't talk to you. At home, I'm not always [4] t......................... . I hate talking in the morning. My mum thinks I'm [5] m......................... but I'm just tired! I get good marks at school because I'm [6] h......................... – I study about three or four hours every day.

James, my best friend, only studies an hour a day. But that's not because he's [7] l......................... ! He's [8] c......................... and can understand difficult things. James is a good friend. He's always [9] c......................... and he loves telling jokes. He's also a very [10] g......................... person and he often buys our drinks when we go to the café.

Vocabulary page 108

45

Chatroom — Agreeing and disagreeing

Speaking and Listening

★ **1** 🔊 1.15 **Choose the correct options to complete the conversations. Then listen and check.**

1 A I think I look like Johnny Depp.
  B *I don't think so* / *I agree.* Johnny Depp's got longer, darker hair than you, he's slimmer and he's taller.

2 A I think my sister looks like Miley Cyrus.
  B *You're right* / *I disagree*, they're both beautiful.

3 A Nigel's the nicest person in the class.
  B *I agree* / *That's not true.* And he's also the best student.

4 A Jack's so selfish!
  B *That's not true* / *I think so, too.* He often helps me with my homework.

5 A I don't think Maya is unfriendly. I think she's shy.
  B *I disagree* / *You're right.* She's a nice girl, but she's scared of new people.

6 A Mr McGregor is the best teacher in the school!
  B *I disagree* / *Maybe.* Mrs Harris is better than him.

★ **2** **Complete the conversations with these words.**

agree	disagree	have	maybe
so	true	up	

1 A I think she looks like Angelina Jolie.
  B I *agree*. They're both tall with long dark hair and green eyes.

2 A Hi, Paula. What's .... ?
  B I'm waiting for Sarah. She's always late.
  A That's not .... She's only late sometimes.

3 A I'm going to the beach with Ricky.
  B .... fun!

4 A Martin's very handsome!
  B I think ...., too. He's got nice eyes.

5 A He's stupid!
  B I .... He's just lazy.
  A ....

Speaking and Listening page 117

★★ **3** 🔊 1.16 **Complete the conversation with these phrases. Then listen and check.**

don't	he's moody	I didn't	I don't
I think	~~that's not~~	what's up	

Nadia What's wrong, Jody?
Jody I said hello to Zak this morning but he didn't answer. He doesn't like me.
Nadia [1] *That's not* true. Of course he likes you! He's great.
Jody [2] .... so, too, but why didn't he speak to me?
Nadia Let's ask Carlos.
Carlos Hi, guys! [3] .... ?
Nadia Jody says Zak doesn't like her.
Carlos [4] .... be silly.
Jody But he didn't speak to me this morning.
Carlos Well, [5] .... sometimes.
Jody [6] .... think so.
Carlos There's Zak!
Zak Hi, guys!
Nadia Go on, Jody, ask him about it.
Jody OK … Why didn't you say hi to me this morning, Zak?
Zak Did you say hi? [7] .... hear you. I was listening to my music. Sorry.

★★ **4** **Read the conversation in Exercise 3 again. Match the sentence beginnings (1–4) to the endings (a–d).**

1 Jody thinks   *c*
2 Jody and Nadia
3 Carlos thinks
4 Jody doesn't think

a Carlos is right about Zak.
b like Zak.
c Zak doesn't like her.
d Zak is moody.

★★ **5** **Write short conversations between Diana and Marcus. Use the information below and expressions from Exercise 1.**

1 Diana liked the film. Marcus liked the film.
2 Diana doesn't like the *Twilight* books. Marcus doesn't like the *Twilight* books.
3 Diana thinks Maths is the most interesting subject. Marcus doesn't mind it. He thinks Science is more interesting.
4 Diana thinks graffiti is great. Marcus thinks it's bad.

Grammar Present continuous for future

★ **1** **Complete the sentences with the Present continuous form of the verbs.**

1 We *are having* (have) dinner at my favourite restaurant on Friday.
2 .... (you / see) your friends later?
3 Emily and David .... (not come) to my party on Saturday.
4 She .... (go) to Ursula's house this evening.
5 .... (Daniel / play) tennis with Stewart in the morning?
6 My parents .... (fly) to London next week, but I .... (not go) with them.
7 What .... (she / do) this evening?
8 Who .... (you / meet) after school?

Brain Trainer

Underline the auxiliary verb.

Helen and Mark are seeing Tom this afternoon.
Helen and Mark aren't seeing Tom this afternoon.
Are Helen and Mark seeing Tom this afternoon?
Now do Exercise 2.

★ **2** **Put the words in the correct order.**

1 playing / this afternoon / are / ice hockey / We
We are playing ice hockey this afternoon.
2 am / later / studying / Maths / I / today
   ....
3 isn't / Helen / in the competition / on Thursday / playing tennis
   ....
4 the film on TV / Lucy and Matt / watching / tomorrow night / Are / ?
   ....
5 not / I / going / this afternoon / am / to / my dance class
   ....
6 you and your friends / are / Where / meeting / tomorrow / ?
   ....

★★ **3** **Make questions and answers.**

1 Adrian / do / judo / this afternoon? ✘
   Is Adrian doing judo this afternoon?
   No, he isn't.
2 Tom and Charlie / play / football / later? ✓
   ....
3 Emily and Alex / go / to the cinema / tomorrow? ✘
   ....
4 Olivia / go to Paris / next week? ✓
   ....
5 Kate / sing / in a competition / on Saturday? ✓
   ....
6 you / visit / your cousins / this summer? ✘
   ....

★★★ **4** **Look at Amy's notes. Complete her email with the Present continuous.**

Saturday
morning: go shopping with Mum
afternoon: help Shelley with her homework!
evening: dinner with Aunt Grace

Sunday
morning: take Rob to the park
afternoon: watch football match with Dad
8 p.m. Erica's party with Greg!

New Message

Send

Hi Maddy!

How are you? I can't meet you this weekend, I'm afraid. On Saturday morning [1] *I'm going shopping with Mum*. In the afternoon [2] .... and in the evening [3] .... On Sunday morning [4] .... In the afternoon [5] .... , and in the evening [6] ....

What about next weekend?

Amy

Grammar Reference pages 94–95

Reading

1 Read the article quickly. Write the names of the people under the photos.

(a) .... (b) .... (c) ....

2 Read the article again. Who …

1 is the youngest person?   *Diana*
2 thinks about the future?   ....
3 has got lots of friends?   ....
4 has got two best friends?   ....
5 plays a musical instrument?   ....
6 thinks it's easy to make friends?
   ....
7 doesn't like moody people?   ....

3 Are the sentences true (T), false (F) or don't know (DK)?

1 Adam is a shy person.   *T*
2 Adam's team is playing in a match tomorrow.   ....
3 Adam's friends sometimes talk about girls.   ....
4 Diana's village has got many places for young people to hang out.   ....
5 Diana is a moody person.   ....
6 Oliver and his band practise every day.   ....
7 Oliver thinks animals make the best friends.   ....

The sChOOL magazine

Last month we asked you about friends. How do you make friends? What makes a good friend? Here are your ideas.

> I'm a shy person, but I have lots of good friends. How did I make them? It was easy! You see, I'm a member of the school football team. The boys in the team are very friendly. They love talking about football – and girls! I don't like talking in front of lots of people, but it doesn't matter; when we're together, the others talk and I listen!
>
> **Adam, 15**

> I love meeting new people, but it isn't easy in my small village. We haven't got a sports centre or a cinema. My friends and I meet in the village café. We talk and make plans about our future. They help me when I've got problems and I help them. We laugh and make jokes. I like that. The worst thing for me is a moody friend because I'm always cheerful.
>
> **Diana, 14**

> I love music and I enjoy hanging out with other music fans. I also play the guitar in a band. We're practising later this evening and we usually have fun together. A good sense of humour is the most important thing for me, and my friends and I laugh at the same jokes. But my best friends are my dogs, Bertie and Horace. Dogs are fantastic friends because they always love you, they're always cheerful and they're never, ever selfish.
>
> **Oliver, 16**

Listening

1 🔊 1.17 Listen to Emma and John talking about how they met. Tick the phrases you hear.

He has dark hair. ☐
He was very friendly. ☐
We went to a café. ☐
He bought me a drink. ☐
She had long fair hair. ☐
We enjoy the same things. ☐

2 🔊 1.17 Answer the questions.

1 Where did John and Emma meet?
   They met in the park.
2 Why did Emma fall off her bike?
   ....
3 What two adjectives does Emma use to describe John?
   ....
4 Where did John and Emma go?
   ....
5 Is Emma talkative?
   ....
6 What things do John and Emma both like?
   ....

Writing A description of a friend

1 Rewrite the sentences. Replace the underlined words with the correct object pronouns.

1 We have got darker hair than <u>Sam and Nick</u>.
We have got darker hair than them.

2 They like <u>Rihanna</u>.
....

3 I met <u>Paul</u> in the park yesterday morning.
....

4 You are more handsome than <u>I am</u>.
....

5 Patrick saw <u>Sam and me</u> at the party last night.
....

6 I saw <u>you and your friends</u> outside the café yesterday.
....

2 Underline the object pronouns in the description.

Ⓐ My cousin Samantha is older than me. She's seventeen and I'm fourteen. We've got different personalities but I like being with her.

Ⓑ Sam's tall and slim and she's got long dark hair and big brown eyes. She's a generous person and she's very friendly and talkative. She phones her friends every day and she often goes out with them. She's a cheerful person and she's hardly ever moody.

Ⓒ Sam loves swimming and horse-riding. She wants to have lots of horses one day. She loves them! She also loves music and the music teacher, Mr Morgan, gives her singing lessons after school. Sam thinks Mr Morgan is a great teacher and she always listens to him. Sam's a great singer!

3 Read the description. Match the questions (1–6) to the paragraphs (A–C).

1 Her appearance ....
2 Her personality ....
3 How old is she? ....
4 What does she like doing? ....
5 What is the person's name? ....
6 What relationship does the writer have with her (e.g. friend, sister, cousin, teacher)? ....

4 Read the description again. Complete column A for Samantha.

	A	B
Name of person	Samantha	
Age	[1] *seventeen*	
Relationship (e.g. friend? relative? teacher?	[2]	
Physical description	[3] *tall and slim* [4] .... [5]	
Personality	[6] *generous* [7] .... [8] .... [9]	
Things they like/do	[10] *swimming* [11] .... [12] .... [13] *singing lessons after school*	

5 Complete column B with information about a person you like.

6 Now write a description of the person. Use the paragraph guide from Exercise 3 and your notes from Exercise 5 to help you.

....
....
....
....
....
....
....
....
....
....

6 It's Your World

Vocabulary Environment verbs

Brain Trainer

Remember! Some verbs have two parts:

clean + up   cut + down
throw + away   turn + off

Learn both parts together. Now do Exercise 1.

★ **1** Match the sentence beginnings (1–12) with the endings (a–l).

1 Don't pollute
2 Let's plant
3 Don't throw
4 Please clean
5 Turn
6 Recycle
7 Protect our
8 They cut
9 Don't damage the
10 Save
11 Reuse
12 Don't waste

a the kitchen up.
b all the trees down.
c your old toys away!
d the lights off when you leave the room.
e the water in our rivers.
f some vegetables.
g the African elephant!
h old magazines and newspapers.
i old things. It's cheaper!
j planet.
k environment.
l water.

★★ **2** Choose the correct options.

1 People .... the river and kill the fish.
   a waste (b) pollute c protect

2 Please don't .... those things! They're expensive!
   a damage b protect c save

3 You can .... old things and make new things from them.
   a clean up b waste c recycle

4 We never .... water in my house.
   a damage b waste c protect

5 We .... a lot of food away, but it's wrong.
   a clean b throw c reuse

6 The mother bear .... her babies from danger.
   a protected b damaged c reused

 3 Look at the pictures. What can people do about the problems? Write sentences with these words.

clean up	plant	protect
recycle	~~reuse~~	turn off

We can reuse old shopping bags.

....
....

....
....

....
....

Vocabulary page 109

Reading

★ **1** Read the leaflet quickly. Match the pictures (1–5) to the paragraphs (A–E).

★ **2** Read the leaflet again. Choose the correct options.

1 It *is* / *isn't* easy to save the planet.

2 We should protect *only beautiful animals* / *all animals*.

3 *Some* / *All* people pollute the beach with litter.

4 The leaflet says we should *throw away* / *recycle* old clothes.

5 You *save* / *waste* energy when you don't turn the lights off.

★★ **3** Are the sentences true (T), false (F) or don't know (DK)?

The writers of the leaflet …

1 are students.   *T*

2 think tigers and polar bears are the most beautiful animals.   ....

3 think we should keep the beach clean.   ....

4 think we should throw away our old clothes.   ....

5 think DVDs are good for the environment.   ....

6 think DVD shops at school make money.   ....

★★ **4** Answer the questions.

1 Who do the writers of the leaflet want to share their ideas with?
They want to share their ideas with other students at the school.

2 Which animals are important?
....

3 When you clean a beach up, where can you put the litter?
....

4 What can friends do with their old clothes?
....

5 Where can you start a DVD shop?
....

6 Why is a DVD shop a good idea?
....

7 What do you waste when you don't turn machines off?
....

Green teens!

We want to save the planet. It isn't easy, so we're going to share our ideas with other students in our school. This is our A–Z of 'going green'!

A is for animals. We should protect animals. Not only beautiful animals like tigers and polar bears. All animals. Why not organise a party for friends and tell them about the problem? Explain that it's important to save the animals AND their environment.

B is for the beach. We love the beach in summer but some people leave their litter there. Take a bag with you and clean the beach up with your friends. It's your beach, so keep it clean.

C is for clothes. Do you hate that pink T-shirt with the purple flowers? Does your friend hate her jeans with the gold stars? Maybe your friend likes your T-shirt and maybe you like your friend's jeans. Don't throw old clothes away. Swap them with your friends and get a new look. It's a fun way to recycle clothes.

D is for DVDs. You aren't going to watch your old DVDs again, but you shouldn't throw them away. They pollute the environment. Start a DVD shop at school. It's better for the planet and you can make money for your school!

E is for energy. Do you leave the lights and machines on when you aren't using them? You waste energy like that. Always turn the lights off when you leave a room. Do the same for the TV, the computer, the radio – everything!

Grammar *Going to*

★ 1 **Put the words in the correct order.**

1 going / recycle / to / She / the magazines / is
She is going to recycle the magazines.

2 am / those old computer games / not / to / I /
throw away / going
....

3 going / buy / to / a new TV / are / We
....

4 to / he / going / his old mobile phone / Is /
recycle / ?
....

5 for a test / are / study / the students / not /
tomorrow / going / to
....

6 clean up / Are / going / the beach / they / to / ?
....

★★ 2 **Complete the questions and answers.**

1 A *Is* Neil going to play tennis on Wednesday
afternoon? ✘ (football)
B *No, he isn't. He's going to play football.*

2 A .... Neil and Sandra going to
study on Tuesday evening? ✓
B ....

3 A .... John and Amy going to
watch a film next weekend? ✘ (DVD)
B ....

4 A .... Amy going to buy a book
on Wednesday morning? ✘ (magazine)
B ....

5 A .... Sandra going to watch TV
this evening? ✓
B ....

★★ 3 **Write the questions.**

1 A *What are you going to do tomorrow night?*
B I'm going to <u>play a new computer game</u>
tomorrow night.

2 A ....
B Yes, we are. We're going to <u>watch a DVD</u>
about the environment tonight.

3 A ....
B I'm going to invite <u>all my friends</u> to my party.

4 A ....
B He's going to go home <u>at eight o'clock</u>
tonight.

Should

★ 4 **Choose the correct options.**

1 I throw away plastic bags.
You (should) / shouldn't recycle them.

2 I always go to bed late.
You *should / shouldn't* go to bed early.

3 I've got lots of homework.
Should / Shouldn't I go to the party?

4 I'm scared.
You *should / shouldn't* watch scary films!

5 I don't want these T-shirts.
You *should / shouldn't* swap them with a friend.

★★ 5 **Complete the sentences with *should* or
shouldn't.**

1 The park's dirty. People *shouldn't* drop litter.
2 The planet is in danger. We ....
protect it.
3 Two men are fighting. .... we
phone the police?
4 Jack wants to live in France. He
.... study French.
5 Water is important. We .... waste it.
6 Sharon is always tired. She .... go
to bed late.

★★★ 6 **Complete the advice with *should/shouldn't*
and these verbs.**

ask	copy	do	~~eat~~
go	recycle	start	stay

1 A I love chocolate!
B But you *shouldn't eat* it every day.

2 A I never watch these old DVDs. What
.... I .... with them?
B You .... them.

3 A I can't do my homework. ....
I .... my friend's homework?
B No, you .... your teacher
about it.

4 A Where..................... we ....
for our holidays?
B I think you .... with your
cousins in Italy.

5 A I've got a lot of homework.
B You .... it now.

Grammar Reference pages 96–97

Vocabulary Materials and containers

★ **1** Match the photos to these words.

cardboard	~~glass~~	metal
paper	plastic	wooden

glass

....

....

....

....

....

★ **2** Choose the correct options.

a *paper / glass* jar

a *wooden / plastic* box

a *cardboard / metal* box

a *cardboard / metal* can

a *plastic / paper* bag

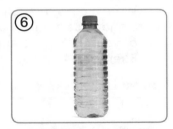

a *plastic / paper* bottle

★★ **3** Put the letters in the correct order. Complete the sentences.

1 Can I have a *bottle* of water, please? (tltboe)

2 We don't like using .... bags. (sictlpa)

3 I'm going to buy a .... of milk. (tnrcao)

4 When they moved house, they put their books in cardboard .... (xboes)

5 Jamie keeps sweets in a glass .... in his bedroom. (rja)

6 You shouldn't throw away .... bags. You can recycle them. (reppa)

7 My little brother likes playing with small .... toys. (dowone)

8 The coffee is in a .... box. (teaml)

★★★ **4** Look at the pictures. Complete the text.

We're a green family! Every week my dad recycles ¹metal cans and ² .... Mum never puts ³ .... in the bin. She always reuses them. We also reuse ⁴ .... and ⁵ .... We don't always recycle ⁶ .... and ⁷ .... because my little brother loves making things from them.

Vocabulary page 109

 **Shopping**

Speaking and Listening

★ 1)) 1.18 **Match the statements and questions (1–5) to the responses (a–e). Then and listen and check.**

1 How much is this T-shirt?   *d*
2 Excuse me, have you got any recycled paper notebooks?
3 Good morning. Can I help you?
4 The wooden elephants are £135.
5 Can I see the wooden box over there?

a They're expensive! I don't want them, thanks.
b No, but we've got these beautiful ones from South Africa.
c Yes, please. I want to buy a cheap digital camera.
d £8.
e Here you are.

★ 2 **Complete the sentences with one word in each gap.**

1 Hello. .... I help you?
2 Have you got .... cheap laptops?
3 How .... is it?
4 That's cheap. I'll .... it.
5 I don't want it, ... It's very expensive.

 Brain Trainer

Match the prices to the words:

£19.99	twenty-eight pounds fifty
95p	nineteen pounds ninety-nine
£9	ninety-five pence
£28.50	nine pounds

Now do Exercise 3.

★★ 3)) 1.19 **Complete the conversation with these words and phrases. Then listen and check.**

£8.50	awesome	can I help
expensive	here you are	how much is it
~~stuff~~	we'll take it	

Nadia	This is an amazing shop.
Jody	This ¹ *stuff* is from all over the world.
Nadia	And look at those big bags. They're ² .... !
Jody	Yeah, but they're ³ .... ! This blue bag's £45.99!
Assistant	Hi. ⁴ .... you?
Nadia	Have you got any cheaper bags?
Assistant	Sure. ⁵ .... What do you think of these sports bags?
Jody	Hmm. This bag's from Chicago.
Assistant	Yes. They recycle old sports shirts to make these bags. This was a Chicago Bears football shirt.
Nadia	Zak's from Chicago. Why don't we buy him this sports bag?
Jody	Great idea. ⁶ .... ?
Assistant	It's ⁷ ....
Nadia	That's cheap. ⁸ .... !

★★ 4 **Read the conversation in Exercise 3 again. Answer the questions.**

1 Where do the things in the shop come from? *They come from all over the world.*
2 What does Nadia think of the big bags?
....
3 How much is the blue bag?
....
4 Where is the sports bag from?
....
5 Why is the sports bag a good present for Zak?
....

★★ 5 **Write a conversation between a customer and a shop assistant. You can use the ideas below or your own ideas and expressions from Exercises 1 and 3.**

book: £5.99   laptop: £399.99   jeans: £14.50

Speaking and Listening page 118

Grammar *Must/Mustn't*

★ 1 Put the words in the correct order.

1 shout / mustn't / in class / You
You mustn't shout in class.

2 must / every day / sport / We / do
....

3 some vegetables / must / He / buy
....

4 They / wake / mustn't / the baby
....

5 on the grass / We / walk / mustn't
....

6 her bedroom / must / She / tidy / now
....

★ 2 Look at the park rules. Complete the sentences with *must* or *mustn't*.

1 You *mustn't* play ball games.
2 You .... take your litter home with you.
3 Parents .... stay with their children.
4 Children .... go into the water.
5 You .... spray graffiti on park walls.
6 Skateboarders .... stay in the skate park.

★★ 3 Write sentences with *must* or *mustn't*.

1 you / copy / your friend's / homework ✘
You mustn't copy your friend's homework.

2 they / drink / water / from the river ✘
....

3 I / learn / the new vocabulary ✔
....

4 she / eat / a lot of sweets and cakes ✘
....

5 he / wash / his hands / before dinner ✔
....

6 you / take / photos / in the museum ✘
....

★★ 4 Look at the poster. Write six school rules.

1 You must be in your classroom at half past eight.

Grammar Reference pages 96–97

Reading

1 Read the text quickly. What kind of text is it?

  a an article in a newspaper
  b an email to a friend
  c an interview in a magazine

Green News

In this week's magazine, meet Tom Baxter. Tom is a member of a group called Green and Clean.

• Hi, Tom. Tell us about Green and Clean.

Well, we're a group of students aged thirteen to eighteen and we want to save the planet. One way to do this is to clean up the litter around us.

• Why is this important for you?

Well, I enjoy mountain biking in the countryside, but I see a lot of litter there. People go walking in the countryside and they leave their glass bottles, paper, metal cans and plastic bags. Litter is dangerous because it can start fires in hot weather. It can also kill – animals and birds sometimes eat it or cut their feet on the glass and metal. Then they get sick and they sometimes die. Plastic bottles are also a problem. They pollute the planet!

• So what does your group do?

We clean up a different area every week. We put the litter in four bins: there's one for plastic, one for metal, one for glass and one for paper. Then we take the bins to the recycling centre.

• Is litter the biggest problem for the environment?

No, there are bigger problems and we can help the environment in other ways, too. We should use bicycles, not cars, because bicycles don't pollute the environment. We shouldn't waste food, water and energy. We should protect wild animals and their environment. And, of course, we should reuse and recycle things, not throw them away.

2 Read the text again. Answer the questions.

  1 Find the names of four containers.
    bottles, ...

  2 Tom gives three reasons why litter is bad for the environment. List them.
    ....
    ....
    ....

  3 Tom talks about four ways people can protect the environment. List them.
    ....
    ....
    ....
    ....

3 Match the sentence beginnings (1–6) to the endings (a–f).

  1 Tom sees a lot of litter   *f*
  2 Tom talks about
  3 Litter can start
  4 Litter can make
  5 Plastic bottles
  6 The members of Green and Clean

  a fires in the countryside.
  b four kinds of litter.
  c animals and birds sick.
  d pollute the environment.
  e take the litter to a recycling centre.
  f when he goes mountain biking.

Listening

1 🔊 1.20 Listen to Sandra and Richard shopping. Tick the things they see.

  a hat ☐   notebooks ☐
  chocolate ☐   clocks ☐
  CDs ☐

2 🔊 1.20 Listen again. Choose the correct options.

  1 The hat costs .... .
    a £13   **b** £30   **c** £33

  2 They use .... to make the hats and belts.
    a paper   **b** plastic   **c** metal

  3 The bike is in a .... box.
    a metal   **b** plastic   **c** cardboard

  4 They used .... cans to make the bike.
    a 285   **b** 2,850   **c** 85

  5 Richard buys the .... .
    a chocolate   **b** bike   **c** notebook

Writing An information leaflet

1 Match the sentence beginnings (1–3) to the endings (a–c).

1 Most people in Britain use
2 Water covers about 71%
3 One person in eight

a doesn't drink clean water.
b about 150 litres of water every day.
c of the Earth's surface.

2 Read the leaflet. Match the headings (A–D) to the paragraphs (1–4).

A What is Cleaner Water going to do?
B Why is water important?
C Why is the water becoming dirty?
D What should we do?

Become a member of Cleaner Water!

Did you know?
Water covers 71% of the Earth's surface, but one person in eight doesn't have clean water to drink.

1 *Why is water important?*
Most people in Britain use about 150 litres of water every day. We prepare food with it, we clean with it and we drink it.

2 ....
We're polluting it. Ships pollute the seas with oil. Factories pollute rivers with dangerous chemicals. People throw away plastic bottles, metal cans and cardboard boxes. This litter gets into rivers and the sea. Oil, chemicals, plastic and metal can kill animals and plants in the water.

3 ....
• We shouldn't pollute rivers and the sea.
• We should recycle paper, metal, glass and plastic.
• We shouldn't drop litter.

4 ....
• We're going to tell people about the problem.
• We're going to organise a green festival at the beach.
• We're going to clean up the beach.

3 You are going to write a leaflet for a group called Amazon Warriors. First, complete the text with these words.

beautiful	burn	cut	destroying
important	millions	people	plant
protect	weather		

The Amazon rainforest is one of the most
¹ *beautiful* places on earth. It is also
² .... for the world's weather. It is the
home of ³ .... of different animals and
about 40,000 different plants. But people are
⁴ .... the rainforest for many reasons.
They ⁵ .... down the trees for wood.
They sometimes ⁶ .... other trees to
make paper, but animals can't live in these trees.
They ⁷ .... the rainforest to make farms
and ranches for cows. The ⁸ .... in
the Amazon rainforest are losing their homes.
The world's ⁹ .... is changing.
Amazon Warriors want to ¹⁰ .... the
rainforest.

4 Now write a leaflet for Amazon Warriors. Use the leaflet guide below and the information in Exercise 3 to help you.

SAVE THE AMAZON RAINFOREST!

Did you know?
About 40,000 different plants and millions of kinds of animals live in the Amazon rainforest.

What do we know about the Amazon rainforest?
The Amazon rainforest is one of the most beautiful places in the world.
....
....

What problems does the Amazon rainforest have?
....
....

What should we do to save the rainforest?
• ....

Become a member of Amazon Warriors!
We are going to:
• ....

Grammar

1 **Complete the text with the Past simple or Past continuous form of the verbs.**

Last summer I ⁰ *was walking* (walk) in the mountains in Scotland when I ¹........................ (see) a beautiful old castle. I ²........................ (take) photos of it when an old lady ³........................ (stop) her car near me and ⁴........................ (say) good morning. She was very nice and we ⁵........................ (talk) together for a few minutes. That evening, while I ⁶........................ (watch) TV, I ⁷........................ (see) the old lady's face on TV. She was the Queen of England!

/ 7 marks

2 **Complete the text with the comparative or the superlative form of the adjectives.**

This year Laura is studying French in Paris, ⁰ *the most romantic* (romantic) city in the world. She is living in a small house. It is ¹........................ (small) than Laura's house in England, but she loves it there. All the students in Laura's class speak good French, but Laura speaks ²........................ (good) French than the others and people sometimes think she is French!

Tonight, Laura and two of her friends, Sandrine and Stephanie, are having dinner in a restaurant. The food here is ³........................ (expensive) than café food, but Laura thinks it is ⁴........................ (tasty) food in the world. She also thinks the ice cream here is ⁵........................ (good) in the city! After dinner the girls are meeting their new friends, Henri and Luc. 'Henri is two years ⁶........................ (young) than us, but he's very nice,' says Laura, 'and Luc's jokes are ⁷........................ (bad) in the world, but he makes us laugh.'

/ 7 marks

3 **Complete the sentences with these words.**

am	isn't	must	mustn't
should	should	t̶o̶	

0 Are you going *to* visit your grandmother this summer?

1 'I don't understand this exercise.' 'You .... ask your teacher to help you.'

2 I .... going to study for my Maths exam tonight.

3 Dad .... going to buy that car because it's very expensive.

4 You .... eat in the classroom! It's a school rule.

5 '........................ I tell my parents about my problem?' 'Yes, it's a good idea.'

6 You can't talk in the library. You .... be quiet.

/ 6 marks

Vocabulary

4 Choose the correct options.

0 Everyone likes Sandra because she's friendly and ..... .
   a lazy   **b** selfish   **(c)** generous

1 When the teacher walked .... the classroom, it was very noisy.
   a into   **b** off   **c** over

2 Alan doesn't like talking to people at parties. He's very .... .
   a clever   **b** shy   **c** cheerful

3 The brothers were .... when their dad came home.
   a fighting   **b** bullying   **c** dropping

4 Paula has got brown eyes and long .... hair.
   a slim   **b** well-built   **c** curly

5 Don't .... metal cans or plastic bottles away. They're dangerous for animals and birds.
   a recycle   **b** protect   **c** throw

6 The friends walked .... the river and talked.
   a on   **b** along   **c** under

7 Jack was .... graffiti on the wall because he was bored.
   a copying   **b** cheating   **c** spraying

8 Ellen wasn't happy when her brother .... to their parents.
   a lied   **b** copied   **c** stole

9 I looked .... the classroom, but I didn't see my bag.
   a through   **b** around   **c** off

10 It's a good idea to buy .... jars and bottles because you can reuse them.
   a wooden   **b** glass   **c** paper

/ 10 marks

Speaking

5 Match the statements and questions (1–5) to the responses (a–e).

0 *Avatar* is a great film!   *f*
1 Do you think I look like my sister?
2 I came first in the competition!
3 I lost my money on the bus this morning.
4 I think Beyoncé is a fantastic singer.
5 The capital of New York State isn't New York. It's Albany.

a Oh no! Poor you!
b Hmm, maybe, but she's got longer hair and green eyes.
c I think so, too. I love her songs!
d That's great!
e That's right, and the capital of California is Sacramento.
f I disagree. I think it's silly.

/ 5 marks

6 Complete the conversation with one word in each gap.

A Good morning. **0** *Can* I help you?
B **1** .... you got the new Justin Bieber CD?
A Yes, we have. **2** .... you are.
B How much **3** .... it?
A It **4** .... £10.
B Oh, that's cheap! I'll **5** .... it, thanks.

/ 5 marks

Translation

7 Translate the sentences.

1 She was copying her friend's homework when the teacher saw her.
2 He ran across the street.
3 Bob is tall and slim and he's got a beard.
4 We must all recycle paper and protect the environment.
5 I bought the most expensive watch in the shop.

/ 5 marks

Dictation

8 🔊 1.21 **Listen and write.**

/ 5 marks

7 Make Music

Vocabulary Music

★ 1 Complete the music words in the puzzle. What is word number 9?

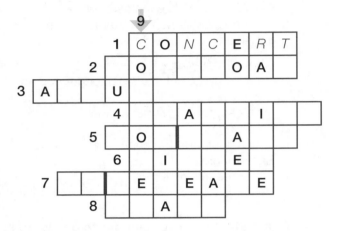

1	C	O	N	C	E	R	T
2		O			O	A
3 A			U				
4				A		I
5			O		A
6		I		E
7		E	E	A	E
8		A

★ 2 Match the words (1–6) to the sentences (a–f).

1 album   *d*
2 composer
3 digital music
4 hit
5 radio station
6 track

a This is music on a computer or MP3 player.
b This is one of the songs on a CD.
c This is a successful song.
d This is a number of songs or pieces of music on a CD.
e This plays music.
f This person writes music.

★★ 3 Complete the sentences with these words.

CD releases	composer	digital music
playlist	pop chart	~~radio station~~

1 Jack is listening to a *radio station* in his bedroom.
2 Can I see the .... on your MP3 player? Oh! You've got some great songs!
3 I want to be a .... and write music for films.
4 You can read about all the new .... in this magazine.
5 Most people download .... from the internet.
6 Which song is number one in the .... this week?

★★★ 4 Complete the article with these words.

album	composer	~~concert~~	download
hits	pop charts	radio stations	singer

A great night for The Chill

There were thousands of people at last night's ¹*concert*. The American band, The Chill, played all their greatest ² .... They also played songs from their new ³ .... *High River*. I think the song *Leaving Home* is going to be in the ⁴ .... very soon. You can hear the song on most ⁵ .... and you can also ⁶ .... it from the internet for 99p. Mark Philips, the band's ⁷ .... , wrote the song. He's an amazing ⁸ ....

Vocabulary page 110

Reading

★ **1** Read the interview quickly. Tick the words that are mentioned.

playlist ☐
digital music ☐
track ☐
pop chart ☐
hit ☐
concert ☐

★ **2** Read the interview again. Choose the correct options.

1 New Groove Radio is the name of *a radio station / Belinda's programme.*

2 Belinda *plays / doesn't play* hits on her programme.

3 She thinks CDs are *cheap / expensive.*

4 She plays *new and old music / new music only.*

5 She thinks people *will / won't* listen to music on the radio in the future.

★★ **3** Match the sentence beginnings (1–5) to the endings (a–e).

1 You can hear music   *b*
2 Belinda says it is important
3 CDs are
4 Some people
5 Belinda thinks

a more expensive than music from the internet.
b from all over the world on Belinda's programme.
c to play music by new singers and composers.
d download music but don't pay for it.
e the best way to listen to music is to go to a concert.

★★ **4** Answer the questions.

1 What does Belinda talk about on her programme?
....

2 Does she play hits by popular bands?
....

3 Why is it important to play music by new singers and composers?
....

4 Why do many people download music from the internet? Give two reasons.
....

5 What does Belinda think is the best way to listen to music?
....

The Future of Music Radio Stations

From the vinyl record and the cassette to the CD and digital music, the way we listen to music is changing. How will we listen to music in the future? Ricky Morris talks to DJ Belinda Roberts.

Belinda, tell us about your job. What do you do?

Well, Ricky, I'm a DJ and I have a programme on a radio station called New Groove Radio. On my programme, I talk about CD releases and I play interesting music from all over the world; not hits by popular bands and old favourites. Every week, I play music by new singers and composers. I think that's important because people can learn about new types of music. Then they sometimes go out and buy the album.

But more and more people don't go to music shops any more.

That's true. CDs aren't cheap, so many people download albums. It's easy to buy music from the internet, but you must pay for it! Some people don't pay; they steal the music and this is bad for music and musicians.

Do you think people will stop listening to the radio in the future?

No I don't. I think people will always listen to music on radio stations. It's the best way to learn about new music. But, of course, the best way to listen to music is to go to a concert. There's nothing better!

Grammar *Will*

★ **1** Complete the sentences with the correct form of *will*. Then write prediction (P) or offer (O).

1 He's the worst dancer in the competition.
He *won't win* (not win).   *P*

2 'It's so hot in here!' 'I .... (open) the window.'   ....

3 Her new album is rubbish. People .... (buy) it.   ....

4 'I forgot to tell Anna about the test tomorrow!' 'Don't worry. I .... (tell) her.'   ....

5 People .... (download) more music on their computers in the future.   ....

6 I can sing, but I'm not very good.
I .... (never / be) famous!   ....

7 'This room is a mess!' 'I .... (tidy) it.'   ....

★ **2** Answer the questions.

1 A Will her new song be a hit? ✓
B *Yes, it will.*

2 A Will we buy CDs in shops in the future? ✗
B ....

3 A Will he make lots of money? ✓
B ....

4 A Will she arrive on time? ✗
B ....

5 A Will they enjoy the concert? ✓
B ....

6 A Will you see them at school tomorrow? ✗
B ....

★★ **3** Write offers with these words.

carry them	~~do it~~
download it	go to the supermarket
make dinner	turn the radio off

1 A I haven't got time to wash the car.
B *I'll do it for you.*

2 A I don't want to cook tonight.
B ....

3 A That music is very loud!
B ....

4 A These shopping bags are heavy!
B ....

5 A That's a great song!
B ....

6 A I need some butter to make a cake.
B ....

★★ **4** Write questions and answers.

1 A we / go / to concerts / in the future?
Will we go to concerts in the future?
B no / we / watch music videos / on the internet
No, we won't. We'll watch music videos on the internet.

2 A her song / be / a hit / in the pop chart?
....
B yes / she / become / rich and famous
....

3 A Mum and Dad / arrive / home / late?
....
B no / they / take / a taxi / from the station
....

4 A your friends / like / the film?
....
B yes / they / love / it!
....

5 A you / finish / your homework / early tonight?
....
B no / I / not finish / it / before ten
....

★★ **5** Read the answers. Write the questions.

1 A *Where will James find a job?*
B I think James will find a job <u>in London</u>.

2 A ....
B I'm sure they'll go to <u>Australia</u>.

3 A ....
B Rachel will meet <u>Andy</u> at the station.

4 A ....
B I think she'll <u>write music for films</u> in the future.

5 A ....
B They'll live in the countryside <u>because they don't like the city</u>.

6 A ....
B I think she'll make <u>a pizza</u> for dinner tonight.

Grammar Reference pages 98–99

Vocabulary Musical instruments, types of music

★ **1** Find eleven types of music in the word square.

H	J	A	Z	Z	A	O	I	M	I
I	T	E	C	H	N	O	O	R	C
P	O	A	C	O	P	E	R	A	L
H	L	P	G	C	Z	Y	L	H	A
O	R	A	P	O	N	P	O	P	S
P	E	G	R	U	C	O	K	I	S
X	G	M	L	N	A	Y	A	L	I
R	G	A	K	T	A	H	O	A	C
B	A	Z	R	R	O	C	K	A	A
H	E	A	V	Y	M	E	T	A	L

★ **2** Label the picture with these words.

drums	guitar	keyboard
piano	saxophone	violin

1 ....

2 ....

3 ....

4 ....

5 ....

6 ....

★★ **3** Complete the sentences with the names of musical instruments and types of music.

1 Emma and her friends love *pop music*. They always listen to the new songs.

2 My brother plays the k....................... and the g....................... . He's a great musician.

3 I don't like h....................... m....................... . It's so loud and I can't understand the words.

4 Do you like h....................... h....................... ? I do, and I love Jay-Z.

5 I'd love to learn the v....................... . I think it's the most beautiful instrument.

6 They're from the United States and they love dancing to c....................... music.

7 I went to an o....................... last night. The singers were fantastic but I didn't understand the words.

8 My parents don't want me to practise the d....................... in the house because they're very loud.

★★★ **4** Read the text. Choose the correct options to complete it.

My name's Anna and I love classical music. My favourite instrument is the ¹.... .

I also love singing and I want to be a singer, but I hate ².... songs. I want to be ³.... singer and I am learning Italian, German and French because the words are often in these languages.

My big brother plays the saxophone and he wants to be in a ⁴.... band. My little sister loves dance music and her favourite is ⁵.... . She also likes ⁶.... , but that's not music, that's just people talking fast. My mum and dad like ⁷.... music! I think all those songs about cowboys and horses are terrible!

1 a heavy metal   **b** reggae   **c** piano

2 a pop   **b** keyboard   **c** saxophone

3 a a rap   **b** an opera   **c** a hip hop

4 a classical   **b** guitar   **c** jazz

5 a drums   **b** keyboard   **c** techno

6 a rap   **b** pop   **c** country

7 a classical   **b** country   **c** reggae

Vocabulary page 110

 Offers

Speaking and Listening

 Brain Trainer

Always read the whole sentence, dialogue or text before you do an exercise.

A: Did you like the concert?
B: I didn't … it. ▓▓▓▓▓

Is the missing word *like* or *mind*?

Now read the complete dialogue:

A: Did you like the concert?
B: I didn't … it. It was terrible.

The missing word is *like*, not *mind*!

Now do Exercise 1.

★ **1** 🔊 1.22 **Choose the correct options. Then listen and check.**

1 **A** I don't feel well.
   B *Can I get you a drink? / No, it's all right.*

2 **A** Can I help you?
   B *Yes, please. / No, thanks.* I don't understand this exercise.

3 **A** I must tidy these CDs.
   B *Can I get you a CD? / Do you want some help?*

4 **A** We've got a lot of homework today.
   B *That's for sure! / Yes, please.*

5 **A** I'm thirsty.
   B Can I get you a drink?
   A *Go for it! / No, it's all right.* I've got some water here.

6 **A** I want to write a song for the competition.
   B *That's for sure. / Go for it!*

★ **2** **Complete the sentences with one word in each gap.**

1 Can / help you?
2 Good luck! Go .... it!
3 Do you want .... help?
4 'Can I help you?' 'Yes, ...'
5 Can I .... you a cup of coffee?
6 'Do you want a glass of water?' 'No, it's all ....'

★★ **3** 🔊 1.23 **Complete the conversation with these phrases. Then listen and check.**

do you want	for sure	it's all right
~~some water~~	will be	yes, please

Jody You don't look well, Carlos. Can I get you [1] *some water*?

Carlos No, [2]..................... . There's a glass of water on my desk.

Jody Are you worried about something?

Carlos Yes, I am. Mum asked me to buy her tickets for a concert. I put the tickets in my bag, but I can't find them.

Jody Your mum [3]..................... angry.

Carlos That's [4]..................... ! The tickets were expensive. I'm going to look for them.

Jody [5]..................... some help?

Carlos [6]..................... . You're a good friend, Jody.

Jody Let's take this glass to the kitchen before we go. If it breaks, there'll be water all over your homework. Carlos! Here are the tickets, under the glass of water.

Carlos That's fantastic! Thanks, Jody!

★★ **4** **Read the conversation in Exercise 3 again. Answer the questions.**

1 Does Carlos want some water?
   No, he doesn't.

2 Whose are the tickets?
   ....

3 Where did Carlos put the tickets?
   ....

4 What is under the glass of water?
   ....

★★★ **5** **Imagine your friend has a problem and you offer to help him/her. Write the conversation between you and your friend. You can use the ideas below and expressions from Exercises 1 and 2.**

I can't find my money.
I don't feel well.
I haven't got time to go shopping.

Grammar First conditional

★ 1 Choose the correct options.

1 If you *become* / *will become* a rock singer, will you be rich?

2 If she comes to the concert, *will she sing / does she sing*?

3 Who *will play / plays* the drums if we start a band?

4 Who will you take with you if you *go / will go* to the party?

5 If he *doesn't like / won't like* guitar music, will he buy the album?

6 We will be late if we *don't leave / will leave* now.

Brain Trainer

In First conditional sentences, first look at the verb after *if*. Put it in the Present simple. The other verb in the sentence is the verb with *will*.

If you .... (not like) the film, we .... (leave).
We .... (leave) if you .... (not like) the film.

Now do Exercise 2.

★ 2 Complete the sentences with the correct form of the verbs.

1 If you *win* (win) the competition, you'll *record* (record) an album.

2 If we .... (buy) the song, we .... (listen) to it every day.

3 They .... (not like) the concert if they .... (not understand) classical music.

4 If she .... (like) hip hop, she .... (love) Jay-Z.

5 If he .... (be) a bad singer, he .... (not become) a pop star.

6 We .... (win) the competition if we .... (practise) every day.

7 If you .... (like) the single, I .... (buy) you the album.

8 James .... (pass) the Maths exam if he .... (study) a lot.

★★ 3 Write First conditional sentences.

1 if / it / not rain / he / go / skateboarding
If it doesn't rain, he'll go skateboarding.

2 if / she / see / him / she / invite / him / to her party?
....

3 my parents / be / angry / if / I / not pass / my exams
....

4 if / I / win / a lot of money / I / go / to Paris
....

5 you / be / late for school / if / you / not hurry
....

6 Dad / drive / you / to town / if / you / ask / him?
....

7 if / Jackie / arrive / home early / she / make / dinner / for us
....

★★★ 4 Complete the email with the correct form of the verbs.

New Message   ⊗

Hi Max!   **Send**

Guess what? I'm singing in a competition this weekend. You [1] *'ll see* (see) me if you [2] .... (come) to the theatre on Saturday. I [3] .... (be) really sad if I [4] .... (not win). If you [5] .... (come), [6] .... (you / bring) your camera? I want some photos! If I [7] .... (win) the first prize, the rap singer Mozo [8] .... (sing) a song with me. How cool is that?

Love,
Sandra

Add Attachments: ⊗

Grammar Reference pages 98–99

Reading

1 Read the music blog quickly. Write the correct names under the pictures.

a

b

c

....

CoolMusic.com

My name is Ben Harvey. I'm a music student and I play the piano, the guitar and the drums. In fact, I play the drums in a rock band. I love all types of music, from opera to rap. But my friends only like rock or heavy metal and they don't listen to different types of music. I think this is silly. In my blog you'll find information about classical music concerts, opera music, country music, new bands and singers. If you really like music, you'll love this blog.

Ellie Francis

I first heard Ellie Francis at a concert in Chicago. Ellie studied classical music but now she's a jazz singer. She often performs with her friends Marty Sherman (saxophone) and Jarvis Mason (piano). Ellie is travelling to this city in December and she is giving three concerts at the Cotton Plantation Club. You should buy your tickets for the concert soon. Now click here and listen to the first track of her new album, *Dreamin' Mississippi*.

Street Noyz

If you like hip hop, you'll love Street Noyz – the newest hip hop group from Ireland. The members of the group met when they were still at school. Rory is the best dancer, but all the boys are amazing. The group became famous when they won a talent competition last year. They practise every day. Watch the video. You'll love them!

2 Read the blog again. Are the sentences true (T), false (F) or don't know (DK)?

1 Ben plays three musical instruments.   *T*

2 Ben's favourite music is rock music.   ....

3 Ben's friends don't like listening to different types of music.   ....

4 Ben thinks his friends shouldn't listen to rock music.   ....

5 Ellie always performs with Marty Sherman and Jarvis Mason.   ....

6 Street Noyz are a hip hop group from Ireland.   ....

3 Complete the text with words from the blog.

Ben Harvey writes a ¹*blog* about all ²..................... of music. He thinks it is important to listen to different kinds of music, but his friends only like ³..................... and heavy metal. In his blog, Ben writes about Ellie Francis. Ellie is a ⁴..................... singer and Ben heard her at a ⁵..................... in Chicago. He thinks people should go and listen to her when she comes to this ⁶..................... . He also likes *Street Noyz*, a new hip hop ⁷..................... from Ireland.

Listening

1 🔊 1.24 Listen to Sarah and Liam talking about music festivals. Which festivals do they talk about? Write Sarah (S), Liam (L) or not mentioned (NM).

The Big Music Festival ☐
Summer Festival ☐
Rock World ☐
Lucerne Festival ☐
Jazz Time ☐

2 🔊 1.24 Listen again. Are the sentences true (T), false (F) or don't know (DK)?

1 The Big Music Festival takes place in a park.   *T*

2 Sarah goes to the festival every year with her family.   ....

3 She doesn't go if it's raining.   ....

4 Liam likes jazz.   ....

5 You can hear musicians from all over the world at the Lucerne festival.   ....

6 Liam is going to play Sarah a DVD.   ....

Writing A singer's profile

1 Read the profile about the singer Justin Bieber. Match the notes (1–7) with the paragraphs (A–D).

Justin Bieber

1 Became famous on YouTube A
2 Sings, writes and plays instruments ....
3 The future? More songs and concerts ....
4 Famous singles – One Time, Baby ....
5 Born: Canada, 1994 ....
6 Acts on TV ....
7 First album My World – Number 1 ....

Justin Bieber

) *Who is Justin Bieber?*

Justin Bieber was born in Canada in 1994. One day, his mum put a video of him on YouTube for his family and friends and he soon became famous. He is my favourite pop singer.

....

Justin Bieber sings and writes his own songs. He plays the piano, guitar and trumpet. He also acts on TV and he is in the film *Never Say Never*.

....

His most famous singles are *One Time* and *Baby*. His first album, *My World*, went straight to number one.

....

I think Justin Bieber is great because he's very young. He will write lots of number one songs and perform in concerts in different countries. If he comes to London soon, I'll see him in concert!

2 Read the profile again. Write the headings in the correct place.
1 Who is Justin Bieber?
2 My opinion of Justin and his future
3 More information about Justin
4 Famous singles and albums

3 Think about your favourite singer. Answer the questions.
1 What is your favourite singer's name?
....
2 Where and when was he/she born?
....
3 How did he/she become famous?
....
4 Does he/she play any instruments?
....
5 What is his/her most famous album?
....
6 Is he/she famous for anything else? What?
....

4 Complete this sentence about your favourite singer.
I think [name of singer] is ....
because he/she .... In the future
he/she will ....

5 Write a profile of your favourite singer. Use the paragraph guide from Exercise 2 and your answers from Exercises 3 and 4 to help you.

....
....
....
....
....
....
....
....
....
....
....
....
....
....
....
....
....

⑧ Adventure

Vocabulary The natural world

★ **1** Find the words. Then use the words to label the picture.

beachislandglacierlakemountainwaterfallrivervalleyoceanrainforestdesertsea

1 ....

2 ....

3 *beach*

4 ....

5 ....

6 ....

7 ....

8 ....

9 ....

10 ....

11 ....

12 ....

★★ **2** Complete the sentences.

1 We didn't go swimming at the b*each* because the sea was dirty.

2 Finland has thousands of beautiful l........................ . People do water sports on them.

3 The Mississippi is the longest r........................ in the United States.

4 Emma is studying trees in the Amazon r........................ in Brazil.

5 Mont Blanc is the highest m........................ in Western Europe.

6 Jason sailed across the o........................ in his boat, the *Marie Louise*.

★★ **3** Complete the fact file with these words.

beaches	deserts	~~island~~	mountains	
mountains	ocean	ocean	rainforest	river

Fact file: Australia

Australia is a continent and a country. It is also an [1] *island*, with the Indian [2] .... to the east and the South Pacific [3] .... to the west.

Australia has many [4] .... It is very hot and dry there and in some parts it hardly ever rains.

There are [5] .... in the eastern part of Australia, but they are not very high. The highest one is 2,228 metres. There are other [6] .... in south-western Australia and in the centre of the country.

Water is very important in this dry country and Australia's most important [7] .... is the Darling. It is 1,879 kilometres long.

In the east, there is a small area of [8] .... This is the home of many kinds of trees, plants, birds and other animals.

Australia is famous for its beautiful sandy [9] .... People swim and surf there.

Vocabulary page 111

Reading

Brain Trainer

You don't often need to understand every word in a text. Read the text quickly. Don't stop when you see unknown words. Then write what the text is about in no more than ten words.

Now do Exercise 1.

★ **1** **Read the newspaper article quickly. Choose the best title for the article.**

a Athletics in Africa
b School Athletics Team in Africa
c The Runner – David Rudisha

★ **2** **Read the article again. Choose the correct options.**

1 Maxine is visiting Africa with her school *athletics* / *volleyball* team.
2 The team have been in Africa for two *weeks* / *months*.
3 They *saw some* / *didn't see any* lions in Tanzania.
4 Maxine is learning to *cook* / *dance*.
5 David Rudisha is a famous *runner* / *swimmer*.

★★ **3** **Answer the questions.**

1 Where is the athletics team from?
The team is from Harfield Secondary School in England.
2 Which country did they arrive in?
....
3 What did they see in Zambia?
....
4 What do their Kenyan friends do for the team?
....
5 What are they going to do with David Rudisha?
....

★★★ **4** **Are the sentences true (T), false (F) or don't know (DK)?**

1 Most people in Maxine's athletics team have never visited Europe.   *DK*
2 The team has visited five countries in Africa.   ....
3 Maxine has swum in the Atlantic Ocean.   ....
4 She saw the Victoria Falls in Tanzania.   ....
5 Mount Kenya is the highest mountain in Africa.   ....
6 Maxine enjoys African dancing.   ....
7 Her favourite place in Africa is Kenya.   ....

Amazing African Experience

An athletics team from Harfield Secondary School in England is visiting Africa. Here, 16-year-old Maxine Denby tells us about their trip.

I'm in my school's athletics team and we're travelling through Africa. Most people in the team have never travelled to another continent before and the experience has been amazing!

We left England eight weeks ago. First we flew to South Africa. Then we travelled by jeep to Botswana. After that, we drove through Zambia and Tanzania. In South Africa we swam in the Atlantic Ocean – the beaches there were fantastic! We saw the most beautiful sunsets in the desert in Botswana. In Zambia we saw the Zambezi River and Victoria Falls, one of the greatest waterfalls in the world. In Tanzania we took photos of wild animals – lions, antelope and elephants. Luckily, we didn't see any snakes!

Two weeks ago we arrived in Kenya and we climbed the second highest mountain in Africa, Mount Kenya. We didn't go to the top, so we didn't see any glaciers, but it was still great. We also went to the Great Rift Valley and we went on a boat trip on Lake Victoria. The people in Kenya are so friendly. Our Kenyan friends make special food for us and in the evenings they teach us African dancing. It's fun, but it's very difficult!

Tomorrow is our last day in Africa and it will be exciting because we're meeting David Rudisha. He's a Kenyan and he's a world-famous runner. We're going to train with him and I can't wait!

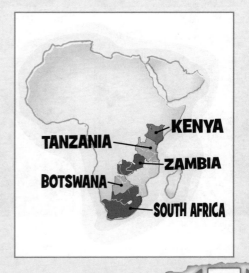

Grammar Present perfect

⭐ **1 Put the words in the correct order.**

1 lions / seen / We / have   *We have seen lions.*

2 my parents / have / I / phoned / today

....

3 read / three books / He / has / this summer

....

4 have / eaten / You / all your dinner

....

5 My parents / visited / have / many countries

....

⭐ **2 Complete the sentences with the negative form of the Present perfect.**

1 We've eaten Italian food, but we *haven't eaten* Mexican food.

2 She's made a pizza, but she .... a salad.

3 I've read the book about Spain, but I .... the book about Germany.

4 They've been to England, but they .... to Scotland.

5 He's called his parents, but he .... his grandma.

⭐⭐ **3 Look at the pictures. Write sentences about Sam's holiday with the Present perfect.**

go / to Italy
Sam has gone to Italy.

he / take / lots of photos
....

he / make / new friends
....

they / climb / Mount Etna
....

⭐⭐ **4 Complete the text with the Present perfect form of these verbs.**

do	go	help	learn
~~make~~	not see	not take	visit

This summer I'm doing a language course in France. I really love it here. I ¹ *'ve made* some great friends and the teachers are fantastic. They ² .... me a lot with my French. I ³ .... a lot of interesting things in France. I ⁴ .... to play boules (that's a French game like bowling) and I ⁵ .... to Languedoc and the Cote d'Azur. I ⁶ .... some beautiful castles in the Loire valley. I ⁷ .... any photos because I can't find my camera! I ⁸ .... the Eiffel Tower, but I'm going to Paris next week!

⭐⭐ **5 What has Charlotte done today? Look at her list and complete the text.**

read about Russia in the eighteenth century ✓
do history homework ✓
visit Gran ✗
go to supermarket ✓
clean the house ✗
call Aunt Vera ✓
write email to Mike ✓
make salad ✓
cook dinner ✗

It's Friday evening. Charlotte has had a busy day. She *has read about Russia in the eighteenth century* and she .... She ....

....

Grammar Reference pages 100–101

Vocabulary Camping

★ **1** Look at the photos. Complete the words.

①
sun hat

②
t _ _ _

③
s _ n _ r _ _ _

④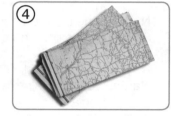
m _ _

⑤
_ _ s _ ct s _ _ _ y

⑥
_ _ mp _ s _

⑦
s _ _ p _ _ _ b _ _

⑧
r _ _ _ sa _ _

⑨
g _ _ d _ b _ _ k

⑩
c _ _ _ f _ _ e

⑪
_ _ r _ h

⑫
w _ _ k _ _ _ b _ _ _ s

★ **2** Write the names of the things in the suitcase.

1 *guidebook*
2 ....
3 ....
4 ....
5 ....
6 ....

★★ **3** Choose the correct options.

1 It's hot. You should use *insect spray /* (*sun cream*).
2 We haven't got a *map / tent*! Where are we?
3 The *guidebook / compass* has photos.
4 We sleep in *rucksacks / sleeping bags*.
5 I'm taking lots of clothes with me. I'm going to buy a bigger *sun hat / rucksack*.
6 'Let's cook dinner.' 'OK, but first we must make a *tent / campfire*.'
7 Oh no! There's a snake in the *compass / tent*!
8 It's dark. I must take the *torch / campfire*.

★★★ **4** You are going to go camping in the mountains this summer. Answer the questions.

1 How are you going to learn about the place? *I'm going to read about it in a guidebook.*
2 What should you take with you so you don't get lost in the mountains?
....
3 What clothes should you take with you?
....
4 What are you going to take to protect your skin?
....
5 How are you going to carry your things?
....
6 Where are you going to sleep?
....

Vocabulary page 111

Chatroom Apologising

Speaking and Listening

★ **1** 🔊 **1.25** **Complete the conversations with one word in each gap. Then listen and check.**

1 A I forgot to buy milk at the supermarket. I'm *really* sorry.
   B Don't .... I'll get some tomorrow.

2 A I'm late. It won't .... again.
   B ....'s OK.

3 A I lost your book. I didn't mean ....
   B It's .... right. I have read it.

4 A I broke the chair. It was an ....
   B These .... happen.

★ **2** **Put the conversations in the correct order.**

a .... Don't worry.
   _1_. You've eaten my last sandwich!
   .... I didn't mean to.

b .... I'm really sorry!
   .... That's OK.
   .... Careful! You're sitting on my camera!

c .... Oh no! It was an accident.
   .... Oh well. These things happen.
   .... You've broken my glasses!

d .... Mum, I broke the living room window. It was an accident.
   .... Don't worry.
   .... It won't happen again.

Brain Trainer

Some words sound the same or nearly the same, but they have different spellings and different meanings. Write words like this in your notebook and learn them. What is the difference between these pairs of words?

there / their   meet / meat   eat / it

★★ **3** 🔊 **1.26** **Complete the conversation with these phrases. Then listen and check.**

| ~~check out~~ | didn't mean | don't |
| I'm really | it was | these things |

Nadia Hi, Jody! What are you doing?
Jody I'm reading an email from my cousin Billy in Australia.
Nadia Is he there on holiday?
Jody No, he lives there. My aunt and uncle moved there four years ago. [1] *Check out* these photos!
Nadia Ooh! He's nice! Is he going to visit England?
Jody Maybe one day.
Nadia Oh no! I've deleted the email! [2] .... sorry, Jody.
Jody [3] .... worry. It's in the deleted items box. We can get it back.
Nadia I'll do it for you. Oh. Jody, I've really deleted it this time. [4] .... an accident. I [5] .... to.
Jody Oh well. [6] .... happen.

★★ **4** **Read the conversation in Exercise 3 again. Answer the questions.**

1 Who is Billy?
   He's Jody's cousin.

2 When did Billy move to Australia?
   ....

3 What does Nadia think of Billy?
   ....

4 Where does the email go when Nadia deletes it the first time?
   ....

5 Who tries to get the email back?
   ....

 5 **Write a conversation between two people. One person apologises for something. The other person accepts his/her apology. You can use your own ideas or the ideas below.**

I forgot your birthday.
I broke your glasses.
I didn't remember to bring you the CD you asked for.

Speaking and Listening page 120

Grammar Present perfect questions

★ **1** Choose the correct options.

1 A *Have /* (*Has*) she visited the island?
B Yes, she *have / has.*

2 A *Have / Has* you been to Mexico?
B No, we *haven't / hasn't.*

3 A *Have / Has* they ever used a compass?
B Yes, they *have / has.*

4 A *Have / Has* he seen this castle before?
B No, he *haven't / hasn't.*

5 A *Have / Has* we sent them an email?
B Yes, we *have / has.*

★ **2** Complete the conversation with the correct form of the Present perfect.

1 A *Have you ever had* (you / ever / have) a bad holiday?
B Yes, I .... I broke my leg last year in Austria.

2 A ....
(you / ever / go) to America?
B No, I .... , but I want to go to New York.

3 A ....
(you / ever / make) pizza before?
B Yes, I .... I love Italian food.

4 A ....
(you / ever / climb) a very high mountain?
B No, I .... , but this year I'm going to the Rocky Mountains.

★ **3** Complete the questions and answers.

1 A *Have they ever stayed* (they / ever / stay) in this hotel? ✓
B *Yes, they have.*

2 A ....
(he / call) his parents to say he's OK? ✗
B ....

3 A ....
(you / ever / eat) at this restaurant? ✓
B ....

4 A ....
(she / ever / go) to Italy? ✓
B ....

5 A ....
(you / do) your homework? ✗
B ....

★★ **4** Look at the picture. Write questions and answers about the boy and girl with the Present perfect.

1 they / bring / sun hats with them?
A *Have they brought sun hats with them?*
B *Yes, they have.*

2 the girl / bring / a rucksack?
A ....
B ....

3 they / had / a drink of water?
A ....
B ....

4 the boy / take / a photo?
A ....
B ....

5 they / see / the sharks in the water?
A ....
B ....

Grammar Reference pages 100–101

Reading

1 Read the article quickly. Complete the sentences.

1 *Luke* is a student.
2 .... is a magazine.
3 .... is a lake in Peru.
4 .... is a drink.

Have you got holiday photos? Send them to *Student Traveller*. If we like them, we'll email you some questions. Your answers will go in our magazine. This week we've heard from student Luke Forbes in Peru.

Hi Luke. Are you enjoying your holiday in Peru?
Yes, I am. Peru is the most amazing country!

What exciting things have you done?
I've been to the Andes and I've seen Nevado Huascarán, the highest mountain in the country. It's 6,768 metres! I didn't climb it because it's very dangerous, but it was fantastic. I've seen the Amazon and I've also walked through the rainforest. It was the best experience of my life and I'll never forget it. The flowers and trees were so beautiful. Oh yes! And I've sailed on Lake Titicaca. That's also amazing. It's on the border of Peru and Bolivia and it's 3,811 metres above sea level!

What about the food in Peru?
I love it. It's so tasty! The people here eat a lot of potatoes, tomatoes and chicken. I've also tried a drink called *Inca Kola*. It's yellow!

Most visitors to Peru visit Machu Picchu. Have you been there?
No, but I'm going back to the Andes next week and I'm going to visit. The Incas built the city of Machu Picchu in the fifteenth century. Some historians think the people there died of a terrible disease. It's really sad.

Thanks for writing Luke. Enjoy the rest of your holiday!

2 Read the article again. Answer the questions.

1 What can you send to *Student Traveller*?
You can send your holiday photos.
2 Which river has Luke seen in Peru?
....
3 What was the best experience of Luke's life?
....
4 What does Luke think of the food in Peru?
....
5 Where is Luke going next week?
....

3 Read the article again. Match the sentence beginnings (1–6) to the endings (a–f).

1 Lake Titicaca is   *b*
2 The highest mountain in Peru is
3 You can travel on
4 Machu Picchu is
5 The Incas built Machu Picchu in
6 Nevado Huascarán is

a a city in the Andes.
b 3,811 metres above sea level.
c a mountain.
d a boat on Lake Titicaca.
e Nevado Huascarán.
f the fifteenth century.

Listening

1 🔊 1.27 Listen to Julia and Mark. Number the items in the order Julia and Mark talk about them.

a mountains ☐
b popcorn ☐
c snowboarding ☐
d a DVD ☐
e a broken leg ☐

2 🔊 1.27 Listen again. Are the sentences true (T), false (F) or don't know (DK)?

1 Mark is on holiday in the mountains in France at the moment.   *F*
2 He broke his leg last week.   ....
3 He broke his leg while he was riding his bike in the park.   ....
4 Mark has got two brothers.   ....
5 Mark wants to come to Julia's house.   ....
6 Julia's got a new DVD.   ....

Writing An informal email

1 Where do you use these words and phrases in an email? Write beginning (B) or end (E).

1 Bye for now. _E_. 4 Hi … ....
2 Dear … .... 5 Lots of love, ...
3 Hello … .... 6 See you soon. ....

2 Read the email. Complete the gaps (1–5) with the correct phrases (a–e).

a Are you having a good holiday?
b I haven't bought her a present
c In the evening we went to the cinema
d we've visited some really interesting places
e I've taken photos of their house and garden

New Message ⊗

Hi Sandra [Send]

¹ _a_. This summer I'm studying English at a school in Brighton! There are students from all over Europe here. We have English lessons every morning from nine to midday, but we don't study all the time. Our afternoons and evenings are free, and ² .... . Check out the photo.

I'm staying with a great family. ³ .... and I'll send them to you soon. The youngest daughter, Lisa, is my age and we often do things together. Yesterday was Saturday and we went to the beach. ⁴ .... . The film was in English and I didn't understand everything, but I enjoyed it!

Tonight I'm seeing some students from school. We're having a birthday party for a girl called Sonia. ⁵ .... , but I've made a big cake for her. She'll love it!

Bye for now.
Emily

Add Attachments ⊗

---

3 Read the email again. Choose the correct options.

1 The email is to *Sandra / Emily*.
2 The email begins with *Hi / Dear*.
3 Emily is studying at a *college / school*.
4 The email ends with *See you soon / Bye for now*.
5 The email is from *Sandra / Emily*.

4 Read the advertisement. Imagine you have been at the school for a week. Answer the questions.

CHURCHILL SCHOOL

Do *you* want to learn good English <u>and</u> make friends from all over the world?

Then come to Churchill School this summer!

There are English lessons every morning. In your free time, you can play sports, visit museums and castles or just relax at the beach.

---

1 Where are you?
....
2 Which activities have you done this week?
....
3 What did you do yesterday?
....
4 What are you doing today?
....

5 Write an email to your best friend. Use your notes from Exercise 4 and phrases from Exercise 1.

....
....
....
....
....
....
....
....
....

9 World Of Work

Vocabulary Jobs

★ **1** Look at the picture. Write the jobs.

1 nurse

★ **2** Complete the jobs.

1 w e b d e s i g n e r
2 f _ _ ness i _ _ _ _ _ _ _ _
3 l _ w _ _ r
4 ar _ _ _ t _ _ _
5 e _ _ _ n _ _ r
6 l _ f _ _ _ _ rd

★★ **3** Who is speaking? Complete the text with these words.

bus driver	engineer
fashion designer	~~fitness instructor~~
lawyer	lifeguard
nurse	web designer

1 I became a(n) *fitness instructor* because I love exercise and I like helping people to keep fit.

2 My job is difficult. I'm a(n) .... and I drive around the city all day.

3 I have the best job! I'm a(n) .... , so I can be at the beach all day.

4 I became a(n) .... because I enjoy working with computers and I really like making interesting websites.

5 I love clothes. I'm a(n) .... , so I work with models.

6 I studied hard to become a(n) .... I make roads and bridges. I'm building a bridge across a river at the moment.

7 When I tell people I work with criminals, they think I'm a police officer. But I'm not. I'm a(n) .... My job is to give advice about the law.

8 Why did I become a(n) .... ? It's great when people leave the hospital and they're healthy!

★★ **4** Write the jobs.

This person …

1 designs things and people wear them. *fashion designer*
2 designs things and people live in them. ....
3 designs things and people walk on them or drive on them. ....
4 designs things and people see them when they turn on their computers. ....
5 helps people in trouble with the police. ....
6 helps people to buy things. ....
7 helps people when they are unwell. ....
8 helps people to exercise. ....
9 helps people in trouble in the water. ....

▶ **Vocabulary** page 112

Reading

★ **1** Read the article quickly. What does Julie make?

    a costumes
    b wigs
    c Italian clothes

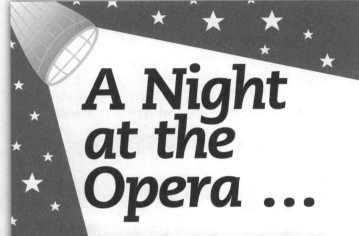

A Night at the Opera ...

This month, Julie talks to us ...

'I was eighteen when I became a hairdresser. I trained in New York and I worked at a famous hairdressing salon for two years. Then I got married and we moved to England because my husband is from here. When I was twenty-six, I opened a salon in London, but after a few years I got bored. I wanted to do something different. Then, one night I went to see an opera for the first time. It was an amazing experience! And the singers had such beautiful costumes and wigs. I thought: 'I can style hair, so I can learn to make wigs!' And I did! Now I design wigs for singers and I also do their make-up.

Next month I'm going to work on an Opera in German, *Der Rosenkavalier*. It usually takes about two weeks to prepare the wigs for an opera, but this project is going to take longer. The opera happens in eighteenth-century Austria. First I must learn about the clothes people wore in Austria in the eighteenth century. Then I'll have a meeting with the costume designer. Together we'll decide the colours and styles for the costumes and wigs. Finally, I'll make the wigs. It's hard work, but I love it!'

★ **2** Read the article again. Choose the correct options.

    1 Julie worked in a New York hairdressing salon for *two / eighteen* years.
    2 *Julie / Julie's husband* is from England.
    3 She opened a salon in *New York / London*.
    4 She *does / doesn't* do make-up for singers.
    5 Next *week / month* she is going to start work on an opera.
    6 The project is going to take *two weeks / more than two weeks*.

★★ **3** Read the article again. Answer the questions.

    1 Where did Julie train to be a hairdresser?
    She trained to be a hairdresser in New York.
    2 What nationality is her husband?
    ....
    3 How old was Julie when she opened her salon in London?
    ....
    4 What did Julie decide at the opera?
    ....
    5 In what century does the opera *Der Rosenkavalier* happen?
    ....
    6 What is Julie going to do before she meets with the costume designer?
    ....

★★ **4** Read the article again. Are the sentences true (T), false (F) or don't know (DK)?

    1 Julie moved to England after she got married.   *T*
    2 She often went to the opera when she was young.   ....
    3 The first opera she saw was an Italian opera.   ....
    4 The story of *Der Rosenkavalier* takes place in Austria and the singers sing in German.   ....
    5 Julie will design the wigs for the singers before her meeting with the costume designer.   ....

Grammar *a/an, some* and *any*

★ **1** **Choose the correct options.**

1 His parents want him to be *a* / *an* good citizen when he grows up.

2 I've got *a* / *some* money in my bag.

3 There's isn't *some* / *any* furniture in the room. It's empty.

4 Are there *any* / *a* programmes on TV?

5 She's *a* / *an* engineer.

6 *Some* / *Any* jobs are very dangerous.

7 He always takes *a* / *an* big black umbrella to work.

8 She didn't want to answer *some* / *any* questions.

9 My little brother is *a* / *an* annoying person.

10 Has your school got *a* / *any* sports equipment?

★★ **2** **Complete the email with *a*, *an*, *some* or *any*.**

> **New Message**
>
> **Send**
>
> Hi Adam,
>
> I'm writing because I need ¹ *some* help. I want ² .... information about architecture and I can't find ³ .... good websites about the subject. Can you give me ⁴ .... advice? Yesterday I saw ⁵ .... interesting programme on TV about famous architects and I've decided I want to be ⁶ .... architect, too. I want to have ⁷ .... good job when I finish school, but now I've got ⁸ .... homework to do and I must study for ⁹ .... test.
>
> Bye for now.
> Josh

★★ **3** **Write sentences with *a*, *an*, *some* or *any*.**

1 there / be / beautiful buildings / in the city
There are some beautiful buildings in the city.

2 I / must / buy / food from the supermarket
....

3 the baby / not have / hair!
....

4 he / drive / electric car
....

5 she / have / good job
....

6 there / be / money / in your bag?
....

Quantity

★ **4** **Choose the correct options.**

1 I've got *a lot of* / *a few* homework today.

2 There aren't *much* / *many* restaurants in our town.

3 He came home, ate *a little* / *a few* food and went to bed.

4 I found *a lot of* / *much* information about lions on the internet.

5 Can I ask you *a little* / *a few* questions, please?

6 You don't need *much* / *many* money to buy this.

★★ **5** **Complete the questions with *How much* or *How many*.**

1 *How much* homework do you have to do today?

2 .... people came to the party?

3 .... information did you find on the internet?

4 .... children do they have?

5 .... money does she have in her bag?

6 .... hospitals are there in your city?

★★ **6** **Complete the conversation with these words.**

a few	a little	a lot of	How many
How much	many	much	much

Anna Dad, I want to be a police officer when I leave school.

Dad Hmm … Police officers work ¹ *a lot of* hours every day.

Anna ² .... hours do they work?

Dad I'm not sure, but they don't make ³ .... money, you know.

Anna Oh. ⁴ .... money do they make a month?

Dad I don't know. Now stop asking questions and do your homework.

Anna I haven't got ⁵ .... homework today. I've only got ⁶ .... Maths exercises.

Dad Listen, Anna. Let me give you ⁷ .... advice. If you don't work hard at school, you won't pass your exams and then there won't be ⁸ .... good jobs you can do.

Anna Oh, all right. I'll start now, Dad.

Grammar Reference pages 102–103

Vocabulary Adjectives
describing jobs

★ **1** Find nine adjectives to describe jobs.

A	D	T	P	B	R	A	X	N	G	H
F	A	S	C	I	N	A	T	I	N	G
A	N	B	R	O	V	Z	Y	S	C	K
C	G	T	V	O	Q	Y	O	T	R	O
R	E	L	A	X	I	N	G	R	E	N
P	R	T	R	O	L	L	T	E	A	R
A	O	Q	I	N	W	I	I	S	T	E
I	U	F	E	O	G	E	R	S	I	X
R	S	U	D	U	L	L	I	F	V	L
S	E	I	M	S	J	D	N	U	E	O
A	R	G	E	I	M	E	G	L	S	D
S	A	T	I	S	F	Y	I	N	G	E

★ **2** Put the letters in the correct order to make adjectives.

1 treufsssl   *stressful*
2 afinngtscai   ....
3 fsigatnisy   ....
4 elwl-diap   ....
5 nagrueods   ....
6 lldu   ....
7 vriead   ....
8 cvaetrie   ....

★ **3** Complete the sentences with these words.

~~creative~~	dangerous	dull		fascinating
relaxing	tiring	well-paid	

1 I'm a fashion designer and I make beautiful clothes. I have a(n) *creative* job.
2 I work in a big bank and I make a lot of money. It's a .... job.
3 I love working in the garden. It's quiet and I can think. It's very ....
4 I take photos of wild animals like lions and elephants. I love my job, but it's ....
5 I stand all day and wash dishes at a busy restaurant. I hate my job. It's .... and ....
6 I love my job. I learn new things every day! It's so .... !

★★ **4** Complete the texts with these words.

creative	relaxing	satisfying	stressful
tiring	varied	~~well-paid~~	

I'm a lifeguard. My job isn't [1] *well-paid*, so I don't make much money. When there are only a few people at the beach, it's [2] .... and I can enjoy the sun and watch the sea, but when there are a lot of people, it's [3] .... because they often do stupid things. I sometimes save people from the sea and this is very [4] ....

I write music for films. People think I have a very [5] .... job – and they're right. I write music for many different kinds of film: action films, animated films, historical films, horror films, so my work is [6] .... But it's also a very [7] .... job because I work for many hours every day. Sometimes I only stop working at midnight.

Vocabulary page 112

 **Reacting**

Speaking and Listening

★ 1 Choose the correct options.

1 A My dog died last night.
   B *That's terrible! / Oh well.* What happened?

2 A I have left my bag at home.
   B *It doesn't matter. / Well done!* I'll give you some money.

3 A Oh no! We have missed the last bus!
   B *Oh well. / That's brilliant!* We can walk home.

4 A I can't come to your party on Saturday. I'm working.
   B *What a shame! / It doesn't matter.* I really wanted you to be there.

5 A My parents are taking us to Canada on holiday this summer.
   B *That's brilliant! / Oh well.* I know you'll have a great time!

6 A I didn't make any mistakes in my homework.
   B *Well done! / What a shame!*

★ 2 ◗) **1.28** Complete the conversations with one word in each gap. Then listen and check.

1 A I've crashed my dad's new car.
   B *That*'s terrible! What are you going to do about it?

2 A I didn't win the competition!
   B What a .... ! I thought your painting was fantastic.

3 A I didn't make any mistakes in the test.
   B Well .... !

4 A My brother came first in the race.
   B That's .... !

5 A I didn't get tickets for the football match.
   B Oh .... You can watch it on TV.

6 A There isn't any orange juice in the fridge.
   B It doesn't .... We can drink water.

★★ 3 ◗) **1.29** Complete the conversation with these words and phrases. Then listen and check.

brilliant	doesn't matter	honestly
oh well	~~terrible~~	well done

Jody Hey, Carlos! What's up?
Carlos Oh, hi, Jody! I was looking for you. I've got good news and bad news.
Jody Tell me the good news first.
Carlos Well, you know my dad lost his job …
Jody Yeah, that was ¹ *terrible*.
Carlos Well, the good news is he's found a really great new job.
Jody That's ² .... !
Carlos There's more. Do you remember the story I wrote for that competition? Well, I didn't win first prize.
Jody ³ .... It ⁴ ....
Carlos I won second prize.
Jody ⁵ .... ! But what's the bad news?
Carlos That *was* the bad news. I didn't win first prize.
Jody ⁶ .... , Carlos! Second prize is great!

★★ 4 Read the conversation in Exercise 3 again. Answer the questions.

1 What does Carlos want to tell Jody?
He wants to tell her some good news and some bad news.

2 What is the good news?
....

3 What prize did Carlos win?
....

4 What is the bad news?
....

★★ 5 Your friend tells you some good news and some bad news. Write two conversations. You can use the ideas below or your own ideas and the expressions from Exercises 1 and 2 to help you.

I got a bike for my birthday.
I didn't pass my exam.
My mum found a really good job.
I lost my mobile phone yesterday.

Speaking and Listening page 121

Grammar Indefinite pronouns

Brain Trainer

Remember the rule:

A person or people: *someone, anyone, no one, everyone*

A thing or things: *something, anything, nothing, everything*

Now do Exercise 1.

★ **1** Match 1–5 with a–e.

1 There's someone outside.   *e*
2 I can see something over there.
3 There's no one at home.
4 There wasn't anything in his bag.
5 I didn't talk to everyone at the party.

a They're all on holiday.
b I only talked to a few people.
c What is it?
d It was empty.
e Who is it?

★ **2** Choose the correct options.

1 *Anyone / Everyone* loved the film.
2 Have you ever met *something / anyone* famous?
3 He hasn't got *anyone / anything* to eat.
4 There is *anything / nothing* in the fridge.
5 She knows *someone / something* with an electric car.
6 There isn't *someone / anyone* at home.
7 She put *everything / anything* in the car.
8 There's *someone / something* in my eye. It hurts.
9 Did you find out *something / anything* about the job on the Internet?
10 Poor Annie! *No one / Someone* went to her party.

★★ **3** Complete the sentences with these words.

anyone	~~anything~~	everyone	everything
no one	nothing	someone	something

1 'Do you know *anything* about computers?' 'Yes, I know a little.'
2 He's a terrible person and .... likes him.
3 He's very shy and he doesn't speak to .... but me.
4 .... stole Dad's car last night, so we called the police.
5 Rachel is very funny and .... laughs at her stories.
6 She's done .... very strange to her hair.
7 The fire burned .... in the house.
8 There's .... wrong with me. I'm fine!

★★★ **4** Complete the conversation with the correct indefinite pronouns.

A Have you heard the news? Some people climbed through a window at the Nelson's house last night and ate [1] *everything* in the kitchen! In the morning, there was [2] .... in the fridge! It was empty.
B Did they steal [3] .... from the other rooms?
A No, they took [4] .... from the other rooms. They also left [5] .... in the right place. [6] .... even washed the plates and glasses.
B Did [7] .... hear them?
A No, [8] .... was sleeping and [9] .... heard a thing. Then, in the morning John Nelson saw [10] .... on the front door. It was a note and it said: 'The food was very tasty. Thank you!'

Grammar Reference pages 102–103

Reading

1 **Look at the pictures. What do you think the website is about?**

  a Stressful jobs
  b Jobs for teenagers
  c Interesting jobs

CoolCareers.com

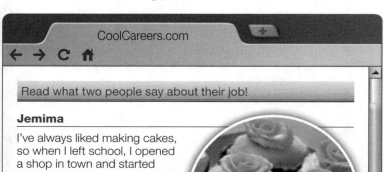

Read what two people say about their job!

Jemima

I've always liked making cakes, so when I left school, I opened a shop in town and started making cakes for parties. I also have a website, so people can buy cakes online.

I get ideas for cakes from flowers, animals, toys, animated films … When I get an idea, I draw it. Then I make it. Next, I take a photo of it for my website. Finally, I take the cake to the customer.

Most parties happen at the weekend, so I work many hours every day, including Saturdays and Sundays. This is not a relaxing job, but I love it!

Gareth

My job isn't for lazy people. It isn't well-paid and it's dangerous. It's also tiring because you can't sit down. So why do I do it? Because I love animals and this is the best job in the world.

I'm a zookeeper and I work with the big cats – lions, tigers and leopards. I often work at night and I sometimes work seven days a week. Every day I prepare the animals' food: I cut the meat in the zoo kitchen and then I carry it out to the animals. That's a lot of meat! I also give the animals clean water to drink, I clean them and I look after their environment. My job is to keep the animals healthy and happy.

Brain Trainer

What are the key words in the questions? Look quickly through the text and find these words, or words with the same meaning. Then read the sentence carefully. This will help you to answer the questions.

Now do Exercise 2.

2 **Read the website and answer the questions. Write Jemima (J), Gareth (G) or both (B).**

  1 Who has a website? ....
  2 Who has a tiring job? ....
  3 Who has a creative job? ....
  4 Who has a dangerous job? ....
  5 Who draws things? ....
  6 Who enjoys his/her job? ....
  7 Who works at night? ....

3 **Answer the questions.**

  1 Where is Jemima's shop?
    It's in town.

  2 What is the first thing Jemima does when she gets an idea for a cake?
    ....

  3 Why does she take photos of her cakes?
    ....

  4 What kinds of cats does Gareth look after?
    ....

  5 Does Gareth make a lot of money?
    ....

  6 Where does he prepare the animals' food?
    ....

Listening

1 🔊 **1.30** **Listen to a radio programme about jobs. Tick the jobs the people mention.**

fitness instructor ☐
waiter ☐
actor ☐
singer ☐
babysitter ☐
lifeguard ☐
nurse ☐
electrician ☐

2 🔊 **1.30** **Listen again. Are the sentences true (T), false (F) or don't know (DK)?**

  1 Felicity lives in California. *F*
  2 Her mother is an actress. ....
  3 Her mother works with famous people. ....
  4 Felicity was working as a waiter a few years ago. ....
  5 The actor's house was next to the beach. ....
  6 Felicity works as a housesitter now. ....

Writing A questionnaire

1 **Each sentence (1–6) has a mistake. Match the sentences (1–6) to the type of mistake (a–f).**

1 Harry studied to be an engineer in the united states.   *a*
2 Mum works at the moment.
3 My job is tiring and I love it.
4 She every day works from eight to five.
5 When did you finish school.
6 'Where is the little boy crying?' 'Because he's sad.'

a capital letter
b linking word
c punctuation
d question word
e tense
f word order

2 **Complete the questionnaire. Do you agree with the advice?**

WHAT JOB IS RIGHT FOR YOU?

Do you know what job is right for you? Find out with our questionnaire.

1 Do you want to go to university?
a Yes, I do.   b I'm not sure.   c No, I don't.

2 Do you want to make a lot of money from your job?
a Yes, I do.
b If I make a lot of money, I'll be happy. If I don't make a lot of money, I won't mind.
c No, I don't.

3 What kind of job do you want?
a I want a fascinating job.
b I want a creative job.
c I don't want a job.

4 Which sentence describes you best?
a I enjoy working with people.
b I want to do something different every day.
c I hate working.

Mostly a answers
A lot of jobs are good for you! For example, you can be a doctor, a nurse, a lawyer, an architect or an engineer.

Mostly b answers
Here are some great jobs for you to think about: a zookeeper, a fitness instructor, a teacher, an artist, an actor, a musician, a cook.

Mostly c answers
You've got a problem! There are many cool jobs in the world, but you must find the right job for you.
Why don't you read about unusual jobs on the internet? Or ask your teachers for some advice.

3 **You are going to make a questionnaire called: *What is Your Dream Job?* Match the question beginnings (1–5) to the endings (a–e).**

1 Why are you
2 What kind of job
3 What is the most important thing
4 Where do you
5 What was/is

a don't you want?
b about a job?
c your favourite subject at school?
d taking this quiz?
e want to work?

4 **Now match the questions 1–5 in Exercise 3 with the groups of answers a–e.**

a A a dangerous job
  B a dull job
  C a stressful job

b A I lost my job.
  B I don't like my job and I want to find a new one.
  C I've finished school and I'm looking for a good job.

c A I want to work at home.
  B I want to travel to different places.
  C I want to work outside: I hate being in a building all day.

d A helping people
  B making or designing something
  C making a lot of money

e A Science
  B History
  C Sport

5 **Three people have completed your questionnaire in Exercises 3 and 4. Which job do you think will be a dream job for each person? Why? Write three sentences for each person.**

Answers for person 1:
1B, 2A, 3B, 4C, 5A

Answers for person 2:
1C, 2B, 3C, 4B, 5C

Answers for person 3:
1A, 2C, 3A, 4A, 5B

Check Your Progress 3

Grammar

1 Complete the sentences with the correct form of the verbs.

0 I'll go (go) to the concert if you *come* (come) with me.

1 If Dad .... (get) home early, he .... (make) pizza for us.

2 The students .... (not pass) their exams if they .... (not study).

3 Who ....(you / ask) for help if you .... (need) it?

4 If it .... (not rain), ... (you / come) to the beach with me?

5 She .... (buy) a new car if she .... (have) enough money.

> / 5 marks

2 Write sentences and questions with the Present perfect.

0 Amy / ever / make / a chocolate cake / ?
Has Amy ever made a chocolate cake?

1 they / never / go / to the United States
....

2 he / not do / his homework
....

3 what / you / do / to your hair / ?
....

4 she / have / many adventures / in her life
....

5 I / see / that film three times / !
....

> / 5 marks

3 Choose the correct options.

0 Put all those things into *a* cardboard box.
(a) a **b** some **c** any

1 Oh no! I haven't got .... insect spray in my rucksack.
a any **b** some **c** no

2 I found .... interesting information on the internet.
a an **b** some **c** any

3 I must go to the supermarket. We've only got .... eggs.
a a lot **b** a little **c** a few

4 I thought I heard .... outside, but I was wrong.
a someone **b** anyone **c** no one

5 She invited .... to her party, but she didn't invite me!
a everyone **b** anyone **c** something

> / 5 marks

Vocabulary

4 Complete the text with these words.

album	downloaded	hit
jazz	~~station~~	track

Yesterday, I was listening to music on a radio ⁰*station* when I heard some amazing
¹........................ music. It wasn't a
²........................ song by a famous rock or pop star. It was a ³........................ from an old
⁴........................ called *Jalousie*. Two great musicians were playing the violin: Stephane Grappelli and Yehudi Menuhin. Of course, I ⁵........................ the music and at the moment I am listening to it on my MP3 player.

> / 5 marks

5 Complete the sentences with these words.

~~guidebook~~	insect spray	mountain
rainforest	river	rucksack

0 Let's read the *guidebook*. It's got lots of information about this place.

1 We walked along the .... and then we stopped to swim in it.

2 We must take .... with us to Africa because there are a lot of insects there.

3 I can't put everything in my .... because it isn't very big.

4 The trees in the .... are very tall.

5 We enjoyed climbing the .... , but we were tired when we reached the top.

/ 5 marks

6 Choose the correct options.

Anne What job do you want to do, Karin?

Karin I'm not sure, but I want to make a lot of money, so I need a [0] *tiring /* (*well-paid*) */ dull* job.

Anne If you become a good [1] *architect / nurse / fitness instructor*, you can make lots of money.

Karin No, I don't want to design buildings!

Anne Well, why don't you become a(n) [2] *lawyer / engineer / web designer*?

Karin No! I don't want to design roads and bridges! Maybe I'll design clothes.

Anne Oh! That's nice! A fashion designer's job is very [3] *dangerous / easy / creative*, but it's also [4] *stressful / dull / relaxing* because you must work very hard and design lots of clothes every season.

Karin Hmm … No, I want an easy job. I think I'll become a(n) [5] *hairdresser / electrician / lifeguard* and sit on the beach all day.

Anne Good idea!

/ 5 marks

Speaking

7 Complete the conversations with one word in each gap.

A I'm thirsty!

B Can I [0] *get* you a glass of water?

A Yes, [1] ....

A I can't go on the trip because it's my sister's birthday.

B What a [2] .... !

A I forgot to send him an email.

B Oh, [3] .... It doesn't [4] .... You can send an email tomorrow.

A I can't find my football boots.

B Do you want some [5] .... ?

A Oh! No, thanks. Here they are.

A I didn't make any mistakes in my test.

B Well [6] .... !

A Mum, I broke your MP3 player this morning. I'm really [7] .... I didn't [8] .... to.

B It's [9] .... right. These things [10] ....

/ 10 marks

Translation

8 Translate the sentences.

1 She will download the track if you ask her.

2 She likes reggae and country.

3 If they go to the mountains, they will take walking boots with them.

4 Please take sun cream and a sun hat with you.

5 She has a dull job.

/ 5 marks

Dictation

9 🔊 1.31 Listen and write.

/ 5 marks

Grammar Reference **1**

Present simple

Affirmative		
I/You/We/They	play	basketball.
He/She/It	plays	

Negative		
I/You/We/They	don't (do not) play	basketball.
He/She/It	doesn't (does not) play	

Questions and short answers	
Do I/you/we/they play basketball?	Yes, I/you/we/they do. No, I/you/we/they don't.
Does he/she/it play basketball?	Yes, he/she/it does. No, he/she/it doesn't.

Wh- questions
What sports do you play?

Use

We use the Present simple to talk about:
- routines and habits.   *He **practises** every day.*
- things that are true in general.   *They **live** in Rome.*

Form

- To form the third person singular (with *he*, *she* and *it*), we add -s, -es or -ies to the verb.
  *She **goes** to the gym.*
- To form the negative, we use *don't (do not)* with *I, you, we* and *they*. We use *doesn't (does not)* with *he, she* and *it*.
  *We **don't play** tennis.*
- To form questions, we use *do* with *I, you, we* and *they*. We use *does* with *he, she* and *it*.
  ***Does** she **like** sports?*

Spelling rules: verb + -s

most verbs: add -s read → reads play → plays	
verbs that end with -ss, -ch, -sh, -x and -o: add -es kiss → kisses watch → watches wash → washes fix → fixes go → goes	
verbs that end with a consonant + y: drop the y and add -ies try → tries study → studies	

Verb + *-ing*

Affirmative		
I/You/We/They	like watching	cartoons.
He/She/It	likes watching	

Negative		
I/You/We/They	don't like watching	cartoons.
He/She/It	doesn't like watching	

Questions
Do I/you/we/they like watching cartoons? Does he/she/it like watching cartoons?

Use

We use *enjoy, hate, like, love* and *don't mind* + verb + -ing to talk about things we like or don't like doing.
*They **enjoy talking** to their friends on the phone.*

Form

The verbs *enjoy, hate, like, love* and *don't mind* are followed by a verb ending in -ing.
*I **don't mind watching** football on TV.*

Spelling rules: verb + *-ing*

most verbs: add -ing   play → playing
verbs that end with -e: drop the -e and add -ing come → coming
verbs that end in one vowel + one consonant: double the consonant and add -ing   sit → sitting

Adverbs of frequency

0% ▬▬▬▬▬▬▬▬▬▬▬▬▬▬▬▬▬▬▬ 100%

never/hardly ever   sometimes/often   usually/always

Use

- We often use adverbs of frequency to say how often we do something.
  I always watch the Olympic Games on TV.
- Adverbs of frequency usually go:
  – before the main verb.
  *I **never** eat pizza.*
  – after the verb *to be*.
  *There is **often** a football match on Saturday.*

Grammar practice
Present simple

1 **Choose the correct options.**

1 My brother *doesn't wear* trainers to school.
   a don't wear **(b)** doesn't wear **c** not wear

2 We .... sport after school on Mondays and Fridays.
   a do **b** does **c** doesn't do

3 .... you play the guitar?
   a Do **b** Does **c** Doesn't

4 Jenny .... swimming every day.
   a go **b** goes **c** don't go

5 .... Sam do sport at the weekend?
   a Is **b** Do **c** Does

6 My friends .... do team sports.
   a not **b** don't **c** doesn't

2 **Complete the questions. Then match the questions (1–6) with the answers (a–f).**

1 ....*Do*.... you like athletics, Jack?   *e*
2 .... Emma like museums?
3 .... they go swimming every day?
4 .... he go snowboarding every winter?
5 .... you play basketball every week, guys?
6 .... it rain every day in England?

a No, they don't.
b No, it doesn't.
c Yes, he does.
d No, she doesn't.
e Yes, I do.
f Yes, we do.

3 **Make sentences or questions with the Present simple.**

1 she / play / ice hockey / after school ✘
   She doesn't play ice hockey after school.

2 what sports / you / like **?**
   ....

3 Max / like / football and basketball ✔
   ....

4 we / do / athletics / at school ✘
   ....

5 Anna and Daniel / run / every day **?**
   ....

6 Jack / go / swimming / every Saturday ✔
   ....

Verb + -ing

4 **Complete the sentences with the correct form of the verbs.**

love: 😍😍   like/enjoy: 🙂   don't mind: 😐
don't like: 🙁   hate: 😠😠

1 I 😍😍 *love watching* (watch) films at the cinema.
2 John 😠 .... (do) athletics at school.
3 The dog 🙂 .... (play) in the garden with the ball.
4 The girls 😐 .... (watch) sports on TV.
5 She 😠😠 .... (wear) trainers.
6 Lucy and Ben 😍😍 .... (go) skateboarding at the weekend.

Adverbs of frequency

5 **Put the adverbs of frequency in the correct order.**

| always | hardly ever | never |
| often | sometimes | usually |

1 .... / 0%

2 .... / ....

3 .... / *always*   100%

6 **Put the words in the correct order.**

1 T-shirts / I / wear / never / to school
   I never wear T-shirts to school.

2 the sports centre / She / goes / often / to
   ....

3 makes / pizza / hardly ever / My mother
   ....

4 a party / is / at the weekend / usually / There
   ....

5 his homework / Sam / on a laptop / always / does
   ....

6 sometimes / on TV / There / a good film / is
   ....

Grammar Reference 2

Present continuous

Affirmative

I	'm (am) watching	
You/We/They	're (are) watching	a cartoon.
He/She/It	's (is) watching	

Negative

I	'm not (am not) watching	
You/We/They	aren't (are not) watching	a cartoon.
He/She/It	isn't (is not) watching	

Questions and short answers

Am I watching a cartoon?	Yes, I am. No, I'm not.
Are you/we/they watching a cartoon?	Yes, you/we/they are. No, you/we/they aren't.
Is he/she/it watching a cartoon?	Yes, he/she/it is. No, he/she/it isn't.

Wh- questions

What am I watching?
What are you/we/they watching?
What is he/she/it watching?

Use

We use the Present continuous to talk about actions that are happening now, at the moment of speaking.
We're **having** breakfast at the moment.

Form

- We form the Present continuous with *to be* (*am, is* or *are*) + main verb + *-ing*.
  *They're **making** pizzas.*
- To form the negative, we add *not* after *am, is* or *are*.
  *It **isn't raining** at the moment.*
- The word order changes in questions: *Am/Is/Are +* subject + main verb + *-ing*.
  ***Are** you **doing** your homework?*
- In short answers we do not repeat the main verb.
  A ***Is** she **eating** popcorn?*   **B** *Yes, she **is**.*

Present simple and Present continuous

Present simple	Present continuous
I often play tennis.	I'm playing basketball today.

Use

Present simple

We use the Present simple to talk about:
- routines and habits.
  I go to the cinema every weekend.
- things that are true in general.
  We enjoy action films.

Time expressions

adverbs of frequency (*never, hardly ever, sometimes, often, usually, always*), *every day, every Saturday, at the weekend, after school, on Wednesdays*

Present continuous

We use the Present continuous to talk about things that are happening now, at the moment of speaking.
She's watching her favourite TV programme at the moment.

Time expressions

now, right now, today, at the moment

Grammar practice
Present continuous

1 Complete the table.

lose	**1** *losing*
2	running
begin	**3** ....
4	studying
look	**5** ....
smile	**6** ....
7	sitting
wait	**8** ....

2 Put the words in the correct order.

1 football / not / at the moment / is / He / playing
He is not playing football at the moment.

2 sitting / We / the shopping centre / in / are
....

3 books / The girls / are / reading / their / now
....

4 Is / at the moment / her homework / doing / she / ?
....

5 smiling / not / You / in the photo / are
....

6 I / a sports bag / not / am / carrying
....

3 Complete the conversation with the correct form of the Present continuous.

Nicole Hi, Adam. ¹*Are you doing* (you / do) your homework?

Adam Yes, I am. I ².................... (try) to finish it because Rafael Nadal ³.................... (play) tennis on TV.

Nicole I know. Dad ⁴.................... (watch) it.

Adam ⁵.................... (Nadal / win)?

Nicole I don't think so. Dad ⁶.................... (not smile).

Adam You ⁷.................... (joke)!

Nicole No, I ⁸.................... . Dad's angry because Nadal ⁹.................... (lose).

Adam Oh no. It's good I ¹⁰.................... (not watch) it!

Present simple and present continuous

4 Read the sentences and write Present simple (PS) or Present continuous (PC).

1 I usually <u>eat</u> *PS* pizza, but I<u>'m eating</u> *PC* pasta today.

2 Jack often <u>does</u> .... judo after school, but he<u>'s studying</u> .... for an exam today.

3 We<u>'re watching</u> .... a comedy at the moment, but we usually <u>watch</u> .... action films.

4 I sometimes <u>go</u> .... to the beach after school, but I<u>'m helping</u> .... mum in the shop at the moment.

5 Charles and Emma usually <u>study</u> .... after school, but they <u>aren't studying</u> .... today.

6 Amanda <u>is sitting</u> .... with me now, but she usually <u>sits</u> .... with Maria.

5 Complete the sentences with the Present simple or Present continuous form of the verbs.

1 Daniel and Anna usually *do* (do) judo after school, but they *are running* (run) in the park now.

2 Sam .... (play) tennis with Fiona today, but he never .... (win)!

3 We often .... (watch) TV in the evening, but at the moment we .... (study) for our History exam.

4 The film director usually .... (make) science fiction films, but he .... (work) on a documentary at the moment.

5 Paula .... (wear) her black jeans today, but she .... (usually not wear) them to school.

Past simple: *to be*

To be: affirmative		
I/He/She/It	was	at the castle.
You/We/They	were	

To be: negative		
I/He/She/It	wasn't (was not)	at the castle.
You/We/They	weren't (were not)	

To be: questions and short answers	
Was I/he/she/it at the castle?	Yes, I/he/she/it was. No, I/he/she/it wasn't.
Were you/we/they at the castle?	Yes, you/we/they were. No, you/we/they weren't.

Past simple: affirmative and negative

Regular verbs: affirmative and negative		
I/You/He/She/It/We/They	lived	in an old house.
I/You/He/She/It/We/They	didn't (did not) live	in an old house.

Irregular verbs: affirmative and negative		
I/You/He/She/It/We/They	went	to London.
I/You/He/She/It/We/They	didn't (did not) go	to London.

Use

We use the Past simple to talk about states or actions that began and finished in the past.
*I **was** at home yesterday afternoon.*
*The war **finished** in 1945.*

Form

- To form the Past simple of regular verbs, we add -ed, -d or -ied to the verb.
- Irregular verbs have different past forms. (See **Irregular verbs**, Workbook page 125.)
- To form the negative of regular and irregular verbs, we use *did not (didn't)* + the main verb in the infinitive.
*We **didn't go** to school yesterday.*

Spelling rules: verb + -ed

most verbs: add -ed *kill → killed*   *visit → visited*
verbs that end in -e: add -d *live → lived*   *die → died*
verbs that end in consonant + y: drop the y and add -ied *carry → carried*   *study → studied*
verbs that end in one vowel + one consonant: double the consonant and add -ed *drop → dropped*

Past simple: questions and short answers

Regular verbs: questions and short answers
Did I/you/he/she/it/we/they graduate from university? Yes, I/you/he/she/it/we/they did. No, I/you/he/she/it/we/they didn't (did not).

Irregular verbs: questions and short answers
Did I/you/he/she/it/we/they see a ghost? Yes, I/you/he/she/it/we/they did. No, I/you/he/she/it/we/they didn't (did not).

Wh- questions
What did he do?   Where did they go?

Form

- To form questions, we use *did* + the main verb in the infinitive. The word order also changes: *did* + subject + main verb.
***Did** she **leave** home when she was eighteen?*
- In short answers we do not repeat the main verb.
A *Did* you *enjoy* the film?   B *Yes, I **did**.*

Grammar practice
Past simple: *to be*

1 **Choose the correct options.**

1 I didn't like the film because it *was* / *wasn't* boring.
2 The students had an exam and they *wasn't* / *weren't* happy.
3 Michael Jackson *wasn't* / *weren't* British. He *was* / *wasn't* from the USA.
4 '*Was* / *Were* you tired last night?' 'Yes, I *was* / *were*.'
5 The queen *was* / *were* in the castle but the king *wasn't* / *weren't* with her.
6 '*Was* / *Were* Megan with her friends?' 'No, she *wasn't* / *weren't*.'

Past simple: affirmative and negative

2 **Are the verbs regular (R) or irregular (I)?**

1 Jack <u>left</u> the party with his friend, Emily.   *I*
2 The boy <u>carried</u> the bike to his house.   ....
3 We <u>stopped</u> at a café in the centre of town.   ....
4 Alice <u>had</u> a good time with her friends.   ....
5 The children <u>saw</u> a ghost in the old castle.   ....
6 We <u>learned</u> about the kings and queens of England last year.   ....

3 **Put the words in the correct order.**

1 enjoy / last night / the party / didn't / I
I didn't enjoy the party last night.
2 left / ago / school / ten / years / My big brother
....
3 in / was / born / nineteenth / the / She / century
....
4 They / to / month / Argentina / went / last
....
5 here / evening / Jake / arrived / yesterday
....
6 in / lots of people / The disease / killed / 1665
....

4 **Write sentences with the Past simple.**

1 John / not have / coffee / for breakfast
John didn't have coffee for breakfast.
2 we / visit / the museum / last month
....
3 Sylvia and Amy / come / to my house / yesterday afternoon
....
4 I / not see / the documentary / on TV / last night
....
5 we / do / judo / at school / last Monday
....
6 the prisoners / not escape / from the dungeon
....

Past simple: questions and short answers

5 **Write questions and short answers.**

1 Mark / like / his new teacher? ✔
  A *Did Mark like his new teacher?*
  B *Yes, he did.*
2 the girls / go / to the library / yesterday afternoon? ✘
  A ....
  B ....
3 Lauren / take / photos / of the castle? ✔
  A ....
  B ....
4 you / do / your homework / on your laptop? ✘
  A ....
  B ....
5 it / happen / yesterday? ✔
  A ....
  B ....
6 she / visit / the museum? ✘
  A ....
  B ....

Past continuous

Affirmative		
I/He/She/It You/We/They	was talking were talking	in class.

Negative		
I/He/She/It You/We/They	wasn't (was not) talking weren't (were not) talking	in class.

Questions and short answers	
Was I/he/she/it talking in class?	Yes, I/he/she/it was. No, I/he/she/it wasn't.
Were you/we/they talking in class?	Yes, you/we/they were. No, you/we/they weren't.

Wh- questions
What were they doing in the library yesterday?

Time expressions

an hour ago   at eleven o'clock   last week
yesterday   yesterday evening

Use

We use the Past continuous to describe actions in progress at a certain time in the past.
*At midnight last night I **was sleeping**.*

Form

- We form the Past continuous with *was* or *were* + main verb + *-ing*.
  *At eight o'clock they **were walking** to school.*
- To form the negative, we add *not* after *was* or *were*.
  *It **wasn't raining** at ten o'clock last night.*
- The word order changes in questions: *was/were* + subject + main verb + *-ing*
  ***Were** the students **playing** truant yesterday?*
- In short answers we do not repeat the main verb.
  A ***Was** Anna **cheating** in the exam?*
  B *Yes, she **was**.*

Past simple and Past continuous

when	while
We were playing tennis when Maria took our photo.	While we were playing tennis, Maria took our photo.

Use

- We use the Past simple for actions that began and finished in the past.
  *We **had** dinner at a great restaurant last night.*
- We use the Past continuous for actions that were in progress at a certain time in the past.
  *We **were having** dinner at eight o'clock last night.*

When and while

- We can use the Past simple and the Past continuous to describe an action that happened while another longer action was in progress. We use the Past simple for the shorter action and the Past continuous for the longer action. To connect the two actions, we use *when* or *while*.
  – We usually use *when* + Past simple.
    *We were laughing **when** Martin **came** in.*
    ***When** Martin **came** in, we were laughing.*
  – We usually use *while* + Past continuous:
    ***While** she **was running**, she dropped her money.*
    *She dropped her money **while** she **was running**.*
- When we start a sentence with *while* or *when*, we use a comma.
  ***While** I **was waiting**, I **read** a book.*

Grammar practice
Past continuous

1 Complete the sentences with the Past continuous form of these verbs.

do	play	sit	talk	watch	~~wear~~

1 Liam *was wearing* a white T-shirt yesterday.
2 The boys .... judo at the sports centre at ten.
3 We .... a horror film last night at eleven o'clock.
4 I .... to my mum when Dad came home.
5 Emma and Laura .... a computer game at four o'clock this afternoon.
6 You .... in the living room when it started to rain.

2 Write sentences with the Past continuous.

1 Max was eating pizza. ✗ (make pizza)
   Max wasn't eating pizza. He was making pizza.
2 Julia and I were watching TV. ✗ (listen to music)
   ....
3 Ben and Daniel were walking. ✗ (run)
   ....
4 I was doing my homework. ✗ (read my emails)
   ....
5 You were walking to school. ✗ (ride your bike)
   ....

3 Put the words in the correct order.

1 last night / was / What / on TV / watching / Emma / at nine o'clock / ?
   What was Emma watching on TV at nine o'clock last night?
2 an exam / Were / this / they / doing / morning / ?
   ....
3 yesterday / Was / playing / football / Billy / ?
   ....
4 having / they / at the party / fun / Were / ?
   ....
5 doing / yesterday / were / What / you / morning / at six o'clock / ?
   ....
6 cheating / Was / Anna / in the exam / ?
   ....

4 Complete the questions and answers.

1 A *Was Daniel listening* (Daniel / listen) to the teacher?
   B No, *he wasn't.*
2 A .... (the girls / play) in the park yesterday?
   B Yes, ...
3 A .... (she / do) athletics at three o'clock?
   B Yes, ...
4 A .... (they / sit) in the café at five o'clock?
   B No, ...
5 A .... (it / rain) at midnight?
   B Yes, ...
6 A .... (Anna / use) her laptop?
   B No, ...

Past simple and Past continuous

5 Choose the correct options.

1 We *left /* (*were leaving*) the bank when we (*saw*) */ were seeing* the thief.
2 While we *sat / were sitting* in the park, a man *stole / was stealing* my bag.
3 When the police *arrived / were arriving*, the boys *fought / were fighting*.
4 He *played / was playing* tennis when the rain *started / was starting*.
5 While Edward *didn't look / wasn't looking*, Max *copied / was copying* his answers.

6 Write sentences with the Past simple and Past continuous.

1 he / watch / a film / when / his dad / ring him
   He was watching a film when his dad rang him.
2 while / they / play / tennis / Jack / arrive
   ....
3 when / I / see / them / they / wear sunglasses
   ....
4 Emma / do / her homework / while / she wait
   ....
5 I sit / in the living room / when / my uncle come in
   ....
6 while / we / walk / to the library / I drop / my keys
   ....

Comparatives and Superlatives

Short adjectives	Comparatives	Superlatives
tall	taller (than)	the tallest
big	bigger (than)	the biggest
large	larger (than)	the largest
happy	happier (than)	the happiest

Long adjectives	Comparatives	Superlatives
popular	more popular (than)	the most popular
interesting	more interesting (than)	the most interesting

Irregular adjectives	Comparatives	Superlatives
good	better (than)	the best
bad	worse (than)	the worst

Use

- We use comparative adjectives to compare two people or things.
  *My hair is **longer** than Angela's.*
- We use superlative adjectives to compare one person or thing to others in a group.
  *Angela's got the **shortest** hair in the class.*

Form

Short adjectives	Comparatives	Superlatives
most adjectives:	add -er small → smaller	add the + -est small → the smallest
adjectives that end in one vowel + one consonant:	double the consonant and add -er fat → fatter	double the consonant and add the + -est fat → the fattest
adjectives that end in -e:	add -r nice → nicer	add the + -st nice → the nicest
adjectives that end in y:	drop the y and add -ier pretty → prettier	drop the y and add the + -iest pretty → the prettiest

Long adjectives	Comparatives	Superlatives
	add more boring → more boring	add the + most boring → the most boring

- After comparative adjectives we often use *than*.
  *Football is **more exciting than** tennis.*
- Before superlative adjectives we use *the*.
  *Jack is **the funniest** boy in the class.*

Present continuous for future

I'm (am) visiting Grandma this afternoon.

They're (are) having dinner with us tonight.

Time expressions

at nine o'clock	next weekend
on Thursday	this afternoon
tomorrow	tomorrow evening

Use

We use the Present continuous to talk about future arrangements.

*I can't come shopping with you.
I'm meeting George at three.*

Form

See Workbook page 88.

Grammar practice
Comparatives and Superlatives

1 Complete the table.

Adjective	Comparative	Superlative
1 bad	*worse*	*the worst*
2 dangerous		
3 easy		
4 exciting		
5 high		
6 hot		
7 tasty		
8 weird		

2 Complete the sentences with the comparative form of the adjectives.

1 *Avatar* is a *longer* (long) film than *Shrek 3*.
2 A Ferrari is .... (expensive) than a Jaguar.
3 Beyoncé is .... (beautiful) than Lady Gaga.
4 The Maths exam was .... (difficult) than the English exam.
5 My cat is .... (fat) than my dog!
6 Maria's got .... (curly) hair than Isabel.

3 Write sentences with the superlative form of the adjectives.

1 Danny / be / funny / person in the class
Danny is the funniest person in the class.
2 Anna and Imogen / good / singers / in the group
....
3 Ben / have got / dark / hair / in the family
....
4 you and I / be / happy / people / in the team
....
5 Naomi / be / clever / student / in our school
....
6 Mark / be / friendly / boy / in the school
....

4 Choose the correct options.

1 Diana's house is *the biggest* in the street.
   a bigger **b** biggest **(c)** the biggest
2 Your English is .... my French.
   a good **b** better than **c** the best
3 The orange juice is .... than the coffee.
   a expensive **b** more expensive
   c most expensive
4 Jack is .... person in his family.
   a short **b** shorter **c** the shortest
5 I think New York is .... exciting city in the world.
   a more **b** most **c** the most

Present continuous for future

5 Write sentences with the correct form of the Present continuous.

1 she / not go / to the cinema / later
She isn't going to the cinema later.
2 you / have / a party / at the weekend / ?
....
3 we / go / skateboarding / this afternoon
....
4 you / come / to the match / on Sunday / ?
....
5 they / not play / tennis / with us / tomorrow
....
6 Henry and Julia / get / married / on Saturday
....

6 Complete the conversations with the correct form of the Present continuous.

1 **A** Hi, Adam. *Are you coming* (you / come) to the park on Saturday?
   B No, I'm not. I .... (play) basketball at school.
2 **A** .... (Adam / go) to the shopping centre in the morning?
   B Yes, he is. He .... (meet) his friends there.
3 **A** Emily .... (not come) to the beach with us today.
   B I know. She .... (visit) her grandma.
4 **A** We .... (not have) a dance class tomorrow.
   B I know. The teacher .... (go) on holiday.

Grammar Reference 6

Going to

Affirmative		
I	'm (am) going to play	a computer game.
He/She/It	's (is) going to play	
You/We/They	're (are) going to play	

Negative		
I	'm not (am not) going to play	a computer game.
He/She/It	isn't (is not) going to play	
You/We/They	aren't (are not) going to play	

Questions

Am I going to play a computer game?

Is he/she/it going to play a computer game?

Are you/we/they going to play a computer game?

Wh- questions

What are you going to do tomorrow?

Time expressions

after school   next week   this summer
tomorrow   tomorrow night

Use

We use *going to* to talk about plans and intentions for the future.
She's going to see her friends this afternoon.

Form

- To form the affirmative, we use *be* (*am*, *is* or *are*) + *going to* + main verb in the infinitive.
  I'm going to do my homework this afternoon.

- To form the negative, we add *not* after *am*, *is* or *are*.
  *We **aren't going to work** together on this project.*

- The word order changes in questions: *am/is/are* + subject + *going to* + main verb.
  *Is your mother **going to drive** you to school tomorrow?*

- In short answers we do not repeat the main verb.
  A *Are they going to play tennis after school?*
  B *No, they aren't.*

Should

Affirmative and negative		
I/You/He/She/It We/They	should recycle	paper.
I/You/He/She/It We/They	shouldn't (should not) recycle	paper.

Questions

Should I/you/he/she/it/we/they recycle paper?

Wh- questions

What should I do?

Use

- We use *should* to ask for and give advice.
  *You **should wear** a hat when it's hot.*

- We use *shouldn't* when something is a bad idea.
  *You **shouldn't throw** those old magazines away.*

Form

- We use subject + *should/shouldn't* + main verb in the infinitve.
  *You **should be** kind.   You **shouldn't fight**.*

Must/Mustn't

Affirmative and negative		
I/You/He/She/It We/They	must listen	to her.
I/You/He/She/It We/They	mustn't (must not) listen	to her.

Use

- We use *must* to talk about rules and things we have an obligation to do.
  *I **must go** home now. Mum is waiting for me.*

- We use *mustn't* to talk about things we are not allowed to do.
  *You **mustn't talk** in the exam.*

Form

- To form the affirmative, we use subject + *must* + main verb in the infinitive.
  *They **must help** their parents with the housework.*

- To form the negative, we add *not* after *must*.
  *They **mustn't forget** their homework.*

Grammar practice *Going to*

1 **Write sentences with *going to*.**

1 Paul / buy / new trainers / tomorrow
Paul is going to buy new trainers tomorrow.

2 we / make / a cake / for Dad's birthday
....

3 Sam and Emily / use / the computer / after dinner
....

4 she / go / to bed / early tonight
....

5 I / visit / my friends / in Spain this summer
....

6 you / start / Spanish classes / soon
....

2 **Write the sentences in Exercise 1 in the negative form.**

1 *Paul isn't going to buy new trainers tomorrow.*
2 ....
3 ....
4 ....
5 ....
6 ....

3 **Write questions with *going to*.**

1 **A** *Is she going to phone Sam tonight?*
B <u>No</u>, she isn't going to phone Sam tonight.

2 **A** ....
B They're going to put <u>oil</u> in that bottle.

3 **A** ....
B <u>Jack</u> is going to clean the living room?

4 **A** ....
B I'm going to leave the party early <u>because I want to go to bed early</u>.

5 **A** ....
B We're going to <u>organise a swap shop</u>.

4 **Complete the conversation with the correct form of *going to*.**

Aiden [1] *Are you going to play* (you / play) basketball this afternoon?

Billy No, I [2]........................ . I [3]........................ (meet) some friends at the beach.

Aiden At the beach? But, it's cold!

Billy That's true, but we [4]........................ (not swim). We [5]........................ (play) beach volleyball.

Aiden That sounds fun.

Billy Then we [6]........................ (have) pizza at the new beach café.

Aiden [7]........................ (Jake / be) there?

Billy Yes, he [8]........................ .

Aiden Then say hi from me. Tell him I [9]........................ (call) him this evening, OK?

Billy Oh, all right.

Should

5 **Give advice. Use *should* and these words.**

| ~~buy / a new camera~~ | not throw / plastic bags / away |
| swap / with a friend | talk / to her about it |

1 **A** These photos are rubbish!
B *You should buy a new camera.*

2 **A** They want to protect the environment.
B ....

3 **A** He doesn't like buying new clothes.
B ....

4 **A** My best friend is sometimes moody.
B ....

Must/Mustn't

6 **Complete the sentences with *must* or *mustn't*.**

1 The film starts at 8 p.m. We *must* be at the cinema at 7:45 p.m.

2 Sandra is at the library. She .... work quietly.

3 People .... use their mobiles in the cinema.

4 I don't want William to know about the party. You .... tell him.

5 The animals are dying. I .... help them.

6 Stop it! You .... eat in class.

Will

Affirmative		
I/You/He/She/It We/They	'll (will) enjoy	the concert.
Negative		
I/You/He/She/It We/They	won't (will not) enjoy	the concert.

Questions and short answers

Will I/you/he/she/it/we/they enjoy the concert?
Yes, I/you/he/she/it/we/they will.
No, I/you/he/she/it/we/they won't (will not).

Wh- questions

Where will they go tomorrow?

Use

We use *will*:

- to talk about predictions or things we think will happen in the future.
  I think he'll win the match. He's a very good tennis player.
- to make offers.
  I'll wash the dishes for you, Mum.

Form

- To form the affirmative, we use *will* + main verb in the infinitive.
  I think we'll buy more music online in the future.
- To form the negative, we add *not* after *will*. The short form of *will not* is *won't*.
  They won't find tickets for the concert.
- The word order changes in questions: *will* + subject + main verb.
  Will people live in big houses in the future?
- In short answers we do not repeat the main verb.
  A *Will her new CD be a hit?*
  B *Yes, it will.*

First conditional

Affirmative
If I have time, I'll (will) call you. I'll (will) call you if I have time.
Negative
If he doesn't finish his homework, he won't (will not) come with us. He won't (will not) come with us if he doesn't finish his homework.
Questions
If they lose the match, will they be sad? Will they be sad if they lose the match?

Use

We use the First conditional to talk about something that will probably happen in the future as a result of another action or situation.
If she doesn't go to the concert, she'll be very unhappy.

Form

- To form First conditional sentences, we use *if* + subject + Present simple for the future action/situation, and *will/won't* + infinitive for the possible consequences of that action.
  If he wins the money, he'll buy a car.
- We can put the *if* clause at the beginning of the sentence or at the end. When *if* begins a sentence, we add a comma. When *if* is at the end of the sentence, we don't use a comma.
  If it rains, I'll stay at home.
  I'll stay at home if it rains.

Grammar practice *Will*

1 Put the words in the correct order.

1 will / in the future / We / live / on other planets
We will live on other planets in the future.

2 books / won't / in the future / Children / from / learn

....

3 in the future / all / speak / the same language / Will / we / ?

....

4 won't / People / music / in / buy / shops

....

5 will / She / one day / a famous singer / become

....

6 buy / People / will / on the internet / most things

....

2 Complete the sentences with *will* or *won't* and these verbs.

~~become~~	love	not go	not win	play

1 I think Sam *will become* a doctor.
2 They .... to France this year.
3 Our school team .... a basketball match on Saturday.
4 Lucy isn't a good dancer. She .... the competition.
5 You .... the new CD from Justin Bieber. It's great.

3 Write questions and short answers.

1 they / win / the match? ✓
  A *Will they win the match?*
  B *Yes, they will.*
2 Anna and Mark / leave / school / next year? ✗
  A ....
  B ....
3 she / become / a teacher? ✗
  A ....
  B ....
4 I / have / a big house / one day? ✓
  A ....
  B ....
5 Luis / buy / tickets / for the concert? ✗
  A ....
  B ....

First conditional

4 Match the sentence beginnings (1–6) to the endings (a–f).

1 If she doesn't practise,   *a*
2 If you go to the party,
3 If she doesn't enjoy the concert,
4 If he goes to the park now,
5 If she takes the bus,
6 If lots of people buy their new album,

a she won't win the match.
b she'll arrive in ten minutes.
c they'll be rich.
d she'll leave early.
e he'll see Cheryl and Bob there,
f will you wear your black jeans?

5 Complete the First conditional sentences with the correct form of the verbs.

1 If I go home now, I *won't see* (not see) Paul.
2 If she goes to Italy, she .... (learn) Italian.
3 If we .... (not like) the film, we'll leave the cinema.
4 If he .... (go) out, he won't finish his homework.
5 If you don't find your tennis racket, I .... (give) you my old one.
6 If Alice comes to the party, she .... (bring) a cake.

6 Complete the First conditional sentences with the correct form of the verbs.

1 If you *go* (go) to bed late, you *will be* (be) tired at school tomorrow.
2 The teacher .... (help) you if you .... (not understand) the exercise.
3 We .... (not watch) the DVD if it .... (be) very scary.
4 If she .... (write) a great book, she .... (become) famous.
5 I .... (stop) them if they .... (start) fighting again.
6 If we .... (win) some money, we .... (move) house.

Present perfect

Regular verbs: affirmative		
I/You/We/They	've (have) cleaned	the house.
He/She/It	's (has) cleaned	

Regular verbs: negative		
I/You/We/They	haven't (have not) cleaned	the house.
He/She/It	hasn't (has not) cleaned	

Irregular verbs: affirmative		
I/You/We/They	've (have) done	the work.
He/She/It	's (has) done	

Irregular verbs: negative		
I/You/We/They	haven't (have not) done	the work.
He/She/It	hasn't (has not) done	

Use

We use the Present perfect to talk about:

- things that happened at no particular time in the past.
  We've passed all our exams!

- experiences.
  I've eaten frogs' legs. They're tasty.
  He's never travelled to another country.

Form

- To form the affirmative, we use have or has + the past participle of the verb.
  My grandma has visited many countries.

- To form the past participle of regular verbs, we add -ed, -d or -ied to the verb.
  watch → watched   arrive → arrived
  study → studied

- Irregular verbs have different past participle forms. (See Irregular verbs, Workbook page 125.)
  do → done   give → given
  read → read   make → made

- The verb go has two past participles: gone (to) and been (to). The past participles have different meanings.
  They have gone to the supermarket.
  = They're at the supermarket now.
  They have been to the supermarket.
  = They went to the supermarket in the past but they aren't there now.

- To form the negative, we use not after have or has.
  I have not finished my homework.

Present perfect questions

Regular verbs				
Have	I/you/we/they	ever	visited	Arizona?
Has	he/she/it			

Irregular verbs				
Have	I/you/we/they	ever	seen	a snake?
Has	he/she/it			

Short answers
Yes, I/you/we/they have. / No, I/you/we/they haven't.
Yes, he/she/it has. / No, he/she/it hasn't.

Use

We use the Present perfect to ask about experiences. We often use ever.
Have you ever eaten Chinese food?

Form

- To form questions, we use: have/has + subject + past participle.
  Has he answered your email?

- In short answers we do not repeat the main verb.
  A Have you spoken to Alex?
  B No, I haven't.

Grammar practice
Present perfect

1 Write the past participles.

1 bring ......*brought*......
2 carry ....
3 do ....
4 feel ....
5 go .... / ....
6 have ....
7 help ....
8 make ....
9 play ....
10 run ....
11 take ....
12 travel ....

2 Complete the sentences with the correct form of the Present perfect.

1 Paula *has seen* (see) the photos in the magazine.
2 We .... (not visit) our friends in New York.
3 Max .... (have) many wonderful birthday parties.
4 It's sunny but I .... (not bring) my sunglasses with me.
5 My sister .... (take) my music magazine.
6 Ben and Jack .... (not play) tennis on this tennis court before.

3 Complete the sentences with the Present perfect form of these verbs.

eat	make	not do
not take	~~not watch~~	visit

1 We *haven't watched* this TV programme before.
2 Sandra .... a lot of new friends at her new school.
3 You .... all the fruit cake!
4 It's late but Oliver .... his homework.
5 I .... a photo with my new camera before.
6 Amy .... her grandma three times this week.

4 Write questions with the Present perfect and *ever*. Then match the questions (1–6) to the answers (a–f).

1 she / win / a competition?
Has she ever won a competition?   d
2 they / climb / any mountains / in India?
....
3 Martin / stay / in an expensive hotel?
....
4 you / see / a famous person?
....
5 you / go / Paris?
....
6 we / have / Italian food?
....

a Yes, he has. He's stayed at the Ritz Hotel in London.
b Yes, we have. We've had pizza and Italian ice cream.
c No, I haven't, but I've seen photos of the Eiffel Tower.
d Yes, she has. She's won a swimming competition.
e No, they haven't, but they've climbed mountains in South America.
f Yes, I have. I've met the actor Michael Douglas!

5 Complete the conversation with the correct form of the Present perfect.

Nina Hi Dan. [1]*Have you seen* (you / see) the new music video with Rihanna? It was on TV.
Dan No, I haven't. I [2]........................ (not watch) TV today. [3]........................ (you / do) your Maths homework?
Nina No, I [4]........................ .
Dan It's really difficult, but my brother [5]........................ (show) me how to do it.
Nina Lucky you! You can help me later.
Dan Sorry, Nina but I'm meeting Amy in five minutes. She [6]........................ (take) some photos for a competition and I'm going to see them.

a/an, some and any

Countable nouns	Uncountable nouns
Affirmative	
There's a child in the park. There are some children in the park.	I found some information on the internet.
Negative	
There isn't a child in the park. There aren't any children in the park.	I didn't find any information on the internet.
Questions	
Is there a child in the park? Are there any children in the park?	Did you find any information on the internet?

Use

- Countable nouns can be singular or plural.
  library → libraries   person → people
- Uncountable nouns have no plural form.
  money, advice, water, information
- We use *a* before singular countable nouns starting with a consonant sound.   *a city, a horse*
- We use *an* before singular countable nouns starting with a vowel sound.   *an activity, an hour*
- We can use *some* before plural countable nouns and uncountable nouns.   *some activities, some money*
- We use *some* in affirmative sentences.
  *I've got **some** tickets for the concert.*
  *I drank **some** water because I was thirsty.*
- We use *any* in questions and negative sentences.
  *I can't see **any** mistakes in the exercise.*
  *Have you got **any** money?*

Quantity

Countable nouns	Uncountable nouns
How many houses are there? There are a lot of houses. There aren't (are not) many houses. There are a few houses.	How much food is there? There's (is) a lot of food. There isn't (is not) much food. There's (is) a little food.

Use

- We usually use *a lot of* in affirmative sentences.
  *There are **a lot of** jobs you can do.*
- We usually use *much* and *many* in negative sentences and questions.
  *I haven't got **much** information about the subject.*
  *Did you get **many** emails last night?*
- We use *How much … ?* and *How many … ?* to ask about quantities.
  ***How much** water did you drink?*
  ***How many** friends have you got?*
- We often use *a lot of* to talk about large quantities and we use *a few* and *a little* to talk about small quantities.
  *We've got **a lot of** homework for tomorrow.*
  *The teacher gave us **a few** Maths exercises.*

Indefinite pronouns

	People	Things
Affirmative	I can see someone. I can see everyone.	I can see something. I can see everything.
Negative	I can't see anyone. I can see no one.	I can't see anything. I can see nothing.
Questions	Can you see anyone?	Can you see anything?

Use

- We use indefinite pronouns to talk about people or things without specifying who or what they are.
  *There's **someone** at the door. Who is it?*
- We use *someone*, *everyone*, *anyone* and *no one* to talk about people.   *We invited **everyone** to the party.*
- We use *something*, *everything*, *anything* and *nothing* to talk about things.
  *The box is empty. There's **nothing** in it.*
- We use *someone*, *something*, *everyone* and *everything* in affirmative sentences.
  *I heard **something** strange in the garden.*
- We use *anything* and *anyone* in questions and negative sentences.
  *I don't like **anything** in this shop.*
  *Do you know **anyone** here?*
- *No one* and *nothing* have a negative meaning, but we use them in sentences with an affirmative verb.
  *There is **nothing** on TV.*

Grammar practice
a/an, some and any

1 Are the nouns countable (C) or uncountable (U)?

1 There's some <u>sugar</u> on the table.   *U*
2 I've got an <u>orange</u> for breakfast.   ....
3 The architect designed a fantastic <u>building</u>.   ....
4 10,000 euros? That's a lot of <u>money</u>!   ....
5 We drink more <u>water</u> in summer.   ....
6 We learned some interesting <u>facts</u> in school today.   ....

2 Put the words in the correct order.

1 haven't / any / got / eggs / We
We haven't got any eggs.
2 some / should / fruit / You / eat / every day
....
3 any / Have / got / water / you / with you / ?
....
4 some / are / on the table / There / magazines
....
5 about interesting jobs / I / find / any / information / didn't
....
6 Has / bought / any / from that shop / she / clothes / ?
....

3 Complete the sentences with *a/an*, *some* or *any*.

1 Paul hasn't done *any* work today.
2 You should read .... articles about the subject.
3 I want to make .... pizza, but there isn't .... cheese.
4 Please give me .... advice. I don't know what to do.
5 Is there .... equipment in that room?
6 This city hasn't got .... good restaurants.

Quantity

4 Complete the questions with *How much* or *How many*.

1 *How many* apples did you buy?
2 .... money did he give you?
3 .... water is there on the table?
4 .... students are there in your class?
5 .... furniture is there in the room?
6 .... friends have you got?

5 Choose the correct options.

1 There aren't *many* shops in this town.
   a much   (b) many   c a few
2 She's given her friends .... CDs.
   a a few   b a little   c much
3 There's .... milk in the fridge.
   a many   b a little   c much
4 There are .... books in the library in town. I think there are about 20,000!
   a a little   b a few   c a lot of
5 I didn't see .... people in the sports centre.
   a a little   b much   c many
6 There isn't .... sugar in this cake.
   a much   b many   c a few

Indefinite pronouns

6 Complete the sentences with indefinite pronouns.

1 The film was great. *Everyone* loved the special effects.
2 Jack isn't here. He's doing .... with his friends.
3 I'm bored. There's .... to do today.
4 There isn't .... to eat at home. Let's go to the supermarket and buy ....
5 Has .... seen my book? I can't find it.
6 We loved the food at the party. .... was very tasty.
7 'Who broke my computer?' he asked, but .... answered him. We all kept quiet.
8 .... stole my bicycle last night!

Vocabulary **1**

Play The Game!

Unit vocabulary

1 Translate the words.

Sports
archery ....
athletics ....
basketball ....
football ....
gymnastics ....
horse-riding ....
ice hockey ....
ice-skating ....
judo ....
mountain biking ....
skateboarding ....
skiing ....
snowboarding ....
swimming ....
tennis ....

2 Translate the words.

Compound nouns
athletics track ....
basketball court ....
football boots ....
football pitch ....
hockey stick ....
ice skates ....
ice-skating rink ....
judo belt ....
swimming costume ....
swimming pool ....
tennis court ....
tennis racket ....

Vocabulary extension

3 Match the photos to the words in the box. Use your dictionary if necessary. Write the words in English and your language.

canoeing   ~~cricket~~   diving   rugby   sailing

1 ..... *cricket* ....

2 ....

3 ....

4 ....

5 ....
....

Vocabulary 2

The Big Picture

Unit vocabulary

1 Translate the words.

Types of film

action film ....

animated film ....

comedy ....

documentary ....

fantasy ....

historical film ....

horror film ....

martial arts film ....

musical ....

science fiction film ....

war film ....

western ....

2 Translate the words.

Adjectives

annoying ....

boring ....

brilliant ....

exciting ....

expensive ....

funny ....

romantic ....

rubbish ....

sad ....

scary ....

tasty ....

weird ....

Vocabulary extension

3 Match the photos to the words in the box. Use your dictionary if necessary. Write the words in English and your language.

| aisle | box office | seat | ~~screen~~ | usher |

1 .....*screen*..... .... 2 ....

3 ....

4 .... 5 ....

Vocabulary 3

Past Lives

Unit vocabulary

1 Translate the words.

History

army ....

castle ....

century ....

die ....

dungeon ....

kill ....

king ....

knight ....

plague ....

prisoner ....

queen ....

servant ....

soldier ....

sword ....

war ....

2 Translate the words and expressions.

Life events

be born ....

die ....

fall in love ....

find a job ....

get married ....

go to university ....

graduate ....

have a baby ....

leave home ....

move house ....

retire ....

start school ....

Vocabulary extension

3 Match the pictures to the words in the box. Use your dictionary if necessary. Write the words in English and your language.

~~crown~~   falconer   monk   peasant   shield

1 ....*crown*....... ....

2 ....

3 ....

4 ....

5 ....

Is It A Crime?

Unit vocabulary

1 Translate the words and expressions.

Breaking the rules

be rude ....

bully ....

cheat in an exam ....

copy someone's homework

....

drop litter ....

fight ....

lie ....

play loud music ....

play truant ....

spray graffiti ....

steal something ....

use a mobile phone in class

....

2 Translate the words.

Prepositions of movement

across ....

along ....

around ....

down ....

into ....

off ....

out of ....

over ....

through ....

under ....

up ....

Vocabulary extension

3 Match the pictures to the words in the box. Use your dictionary if necessary. Write the words in English and your language.

arson   burgle   shoplift   smoke   ~~vandalise~~

1 *vandalise* ....

2 ....

3 ....

4 ....

5 ....

Look At You

Unit vocabulary

1 Translate the adjectives.

Body
short ....
slim ....
tall ....
well-built ....

Eye colour
blue ....
brown ....
green ....
grey ....

Hair colour
black ....
brown ....
dark ....
fair ....
red ....

Hair style
curly ....
long ....
short ....
straight ....

Other features
beard ....
glasses ....
moustache ....

2 Translate the adjectives.

cheerful ....
clever ....
friendly ....
generous ....
hard-working ....
lazy ....
moody ....
selfish ....
shy ....
stupid ....
talkative ....
unfriendly ....

Vocabulary extension

3 Match the photos to the words in the box. Use your dictionary if necessary. Write the words in English and your language.

~~bald~~   mole   scar   shoulder-length   tattoo

1 ....*bald*..........

2 ....

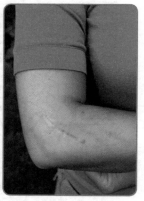

3 ....

4 ....

5 ....
....

It's Your World

Unit vocabulary

1 Translate the words.

Environment verbs

clean up ....

cut down ....

damage ....

plant ....

pollute ....

protect ....

recycle ....

reuse ....

save ....

throw away ....

turn off ....

waste ....

2 Translate the words.

Materials

cardboard ....

glass ....

metal ....

paper ....

plastic ....

wooden ....

Containers

bag ....

bottle ....

box ....

can ....

carton ....

jar ....

Vocabulary extension

3 Match the photos to the words in the box. Use your dictionary if necessary. Write the words in English and your language.

bronze   ~~denim~~   marble   stone   woollen

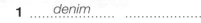
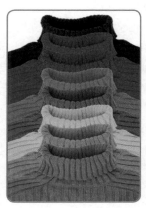

1 ..... *denim* .... 2 ....

3 .... 4 ....

5 ....
....

Make Music

Unit vocabulary

1 Translate the words.

Music

album ....

CD release ....

composer ....

concert ....

digital music ....

download (v) ....

hit ....

playlist ....

pop chart ....

radio station ....

singer ....

track ....

2 Translate the words.

Musical instruments

drums ....

guitar ....

keyboard ....

piano ....

saxophone ....

violin ....

Types of music

classical ....

country ....

heavy metal ....

hip hop ....

jazz ....

opera ....

pop ....

rap ....

reggae ....

rock ....

techno ....

Vocabulary extension

3 Match the photos to the words in the box. Use your dictionary if necessary. Write the words in English and your language.

~~choir~~   conductor   flute   harp   trumpet

1 ...... *choir* .... 2 ....

3 .... 4 ....

5 ....
....

Adventure

Unit vocabulary

1 Translate the words.

The natural world

beach ....

desert ....

glacier ....

island ....

lake ....

mountain ....

ocean ....

rainforest ....

river ....

sea ....

valley ....

waterfall ....

2 Translate the words.

Camping

campfire ....

compass ....

guidebook ....

insect spray ....

map ....

rucksack ....

sleeping bag ....

sun cream ....

sun hat ....

tent ....

torch ....

walking boots ....

Vocabulary extension

3 Match the photos to the words in the box. Use your dictionary if necessary. Write the words in English and your language.

cave   cliff   ~~forest~~   swamp   volcano

1 ..... *forest* ....   **2** ....

3 ....   **4** ....

5 ....
....

World Of Work

Unit vocabulary

1 Translate the words.

Jobs

architect ....

bus driver ....

electrician ....

engineer ....

fashion designer ....

fitness instructor ....

hairdresser ....

lawyer ....

lifeguard ....

nurse ....

police officer ....

shop assistant ....

waiter ....

web designer ....

2 Translate the words.

Adjectives describing jobs

creative ....

dangerous ....

dull ....

fascinating ....

relaxing ....

satisfying ....

stressful ....

tiring ....

varied ....

well-paid ....

Vocabulary extension

3 Match the photos to the words in the box. Use your dictionary if necessary. Write the words in English and your language.

firefighter   florist   pharmacist   surgeon   ~~vet~~

1 ....*vet*........   ....   2 ....

3 ....   4 ....

5 ....
....

Opinions

Speaking

1))) 1.32 **Complete the conversations with one word in each gap. Then listen and check.**

1 A What do you *think* of Sebastian Vettel?
B I .... he's amazing.

2 A .... you like tennis?
B No, I don't. I think ....'s boring.

3 A My .... sport is judo.
B Really? I .... judo, too.

2))) 1.33 **Complete the conversation with these words and phrases. Then listen and check.**

don't	do you	favourite teams	I love
I think	like	~~what do you think~~	

Lily ¹*What do you think* of swimming, Diana?
Diana ² .... swimming. What about you, John?
John ³ .... swimming is boring, and I ⁴ .... like swimming pools. Anyway, I want to watch the football match this afternoon. Chelsea are playing. Arsenal and Chelsea are my ⁵ .... ⁶ .... like Chelsea, Vince?
Vince Hmm. I don't ⁷ .... them, but Arsenal are great.
Lily Right. So the boys can watch football and you and I can swim, Diana.
Diana Cool!

Listening

3))) 1.34 **Listen to the conversation. Are the sentences true (T), false (F) or don't know (DK)?**

1 Alex likes basketball. *T*
2 Maria doesn't enjoy basketball. ....
3 Alex likes horse-riding. ....
4 Maria enjoys horse-riding. ....
5 Alex loves archery. ....

4))) 1.34 **Listen again. Answer the questions.**

1 Is there a basketball game between Spain and Germany tonight?
No, there isn't. There's a basketball game between Spain and France.

2 Does Maria want to watch the basketball game?
....

3 Why does Maria sometimes go to the basketball court?
....

4 What is Maria's favourite sport?
....

5 What is Alex's favourite sport?
....

Suggestions

Speaking

1 ◗)) 1.35 **Complete the conversations with one word in each gap. Then listen and check.**

1 A *What* about asking Helen to come with us to the cinema?
  B That's a good ....

2 A .... don't we visit the Film Museum this weekend?
  B .... , thanks! It's boring.

3 A ....'s watch a DVD at my house tonight.
  B I'm .... ! Which DVD have you got?

4 A Why ....n't we watch the new comedy?
  B .... way! I hate comedies!

2 ◗)) 1.36 **Complete the conversation with these words and phrases. Then listen and check.**

~~come~~	coming	great	let's meet
no, thanks	that's a	way	

Dave What are you doing, Paul?
Paul I'm getting ready to go out.
Dave Where are you going?
Paul To the museum. Why don't you ¹*come* with me?
Dave No ² .... ! I hate museums. Look, what about ³ .... to the sports centre with me?
Paul ⁴ .... ! You hate museums, but I hate sport.
Dave OK. You go to the museum and I'll go to the sports centre. But ⁵ .... at the café later for a chat.
Paul ⁶ .... good idea.
Dave And we can go to the cinema in the evening.
Paul ⁷ .... ! I'm in!

Listening

3 ◗)) 1.37 **Listen to the conversation. Choose the correct options.**

1 Susie and (Marcia) / Adam want to see a historical film.

2 Historical films *are / aren't* Susie's favourite films.

3 Adam *likes / doesn't like* historical films.

4 Adam *wants / doesn't want* Susie and Marcia to watch a film with him.

5 Susie and Marcia *want / don't want* to watch a film with Adam.

4 ◗)) 1.37 **Listen again. Answer the questions.**

1 What is Susie reading?
  She's reading a review about the new Edward Morris film.

2 Why does Susie want to see the historical film?
  ....

3 Who does Marcia like?
  ....

4 What kind of film does Adam want to see?
  ....

5 When does Adam want to go to the cinema?
  ....

Speaking and Listening 3

Reasoning

Speaking

1 🔊 1.38 **Put the conversation in the correct order. Then listen and check.**

   a Well, I don't want to see ghosts.   ....

   b Why?   ....

   c Why not?   ....

   d Because I'm scared of ghosts.   ....

   e Because I love places with ghosts in them.   ....

   f I want to go to the Tower of London.   .1.

2 🔊 1.39 **Complete the conversation with these words and phrases. Then listen and check.**

because x3	don't be silly	don't you
~~say~~	why	why not

Ann It's beautiful here, Sam! Now I want to take a photo of us in front of the castle. [1] *Say* 'Cheese'!

Sam No! I don't want you to take my photo.

Ann [2] .... ?

Sam [3] .... the sun is in my eyes.

Ann Oh, all right. Well, let's walk over the bridge.

Sam [4] .... ?

Ann [5] .... we can see the castle from there!

Sam I don't want to see the castle.

Zoe Cheer up, Sam. Why [6] .... want to see the castle?

Sam [7] .... I'm tired.

Zoe [8] .... , Sam. We can take a good photo there.

Sam Oh OK.

Listening

3 🔊 1.40 **Listen to the conversation. Choose the correct options.**

   1 Barbara is *at home*.

     ⓐ at home   **b** at school   **c** at the cinema

   2 Barbara is watching .... .

     a a historical film   **b** a documentary

     c a film about wildlife

   3 Walter is Barbara's .... .

     a father   **b** teacher   **c** brother

4 🔊 1.40 **Listen again. Answer the questions.**

   1 What is the TV programme about?

     The TV programme is about the plague in the fourteenth century.

   2 Who doesn't want to watch the programme?

     ....

   3 What does Barbara think of the programme?

     ....

   4 Why does Walter hate rats?

     ....

   5 When is Walter's history test?

     ....

Showing interest

Speaking

1 ◗) 1.41 **Choose the correct options. Then listen and check.**

1 A I've got two tickets for the rock concert on Friday.
  B *That's great!* / *Poor you!* Do you want to take me with you?

2 A I can't come to the park with you. I've got a lot of homework.
  B *Oh no!* / *Really?* I don't want to go alone.

3 A I saw Rafa Nadal in the street yesterday.
  B *Really?* / *That's amazing!* You are lucky!

4 A I think a thief took my mobile phone.
  B *Really?* / *Poor you!* Are you sure you didn't leave it at home?

2 ◗) 1.42 **Complete the conversation with these words and phrases. Then listen and check.**

at last	never	poor	really	that's great

Josh Hi, Eva! I've got something to tell you!
Eva Josh! ¹ *At last!* Why are you late? And what happened to your eye?
Josh I fell.
Eva ² .... you! Does your eye hurt?
Josh No, but I broke my sunglasses.
Eva Oh no! How did it happen?
Josh You'll ³ .... guess. I was at the train station when I saw a man taking a lady's purse from her bag.
Eva ⁴ .... ? What did you do?
Josh I ran after him but while I was running, I fell over a small dog.
Eva Did you catch the thief?
Josh No, I didn't. A police officer caught him, but the old lady thanked me anyway and gave me £10.
Eva ⁵ .... !

Listening

3 ◗) 1.43 **Listen to the conversation. Answer the questions.**

1 Who was waiting for Erica?
  Charlie was waiting for her.

2 Who saw Erica in town?
  ....

3 Who was angry with Erica?
  ....

4 Whose party can't Erica go to?
  ....

4 ◗) 1.43 **Listen again. Are the sentences true (T), false (F) or don't know (DK)?**

1 Erica didn't go to her science lesson today. *T*
2 She went to her English lesson today. ....
3 She was in a café when her teacher saw her. ....
4 She often plays truant. ....
5 Charlie knows Jim. ....

Agreeing and disagreeing

Speaking

1))) 1.44 **Complete the conversations with one word in each gap. Then listen and check.**

1 A I think I look like Orlando Bloom, the film star.
   B Hmm, *maybe*. He's dark and you're dark, but he's more handsome than you!
   A That's not .... !

2 A Uncle Jack's a very generous person.
   B I .... He's also very clever.

3 A Mary is unfriendly.
   B I don't think .... I think she's shy.

4 A That was a bad film.
   B I .... The actors were great!

2))) 1.45 **Complete the conversation with these words and phrases. Then listen and check.**

agree	have fun	I think so	maybe
not true	that's right	~~what's up~~	

Cathy ¹*What's up*, Alice? Who are you waiting for?
Alice My brother, Nigel. He's always late.
Martha That's ² .... He's never late for football practice.
Alice Well, ³ .... , but he's late for everything else! We've got a piano lesson at three and it's two minutes to three now!
Cathy I think you're lucky to have a brother like Nigel.
Martha ⁴ .... , too. He's so good-looking!
Cathy I ⁵ .... And he's funny and clever.
Martha ⁶ .... ! And he's the best player in the school team.
Alice At last! There he is. Bye!
Martha Bye, and ⁷ .... at your piano lesson!

Listening

3))) 1.46 **Listen to the conversation. Are the sentences true (T), false (F) or don't know (DK)?**

1 Harry thinks Bobby Rickman is good-looking.   *F*
2 His mother thinks Bobby Rickman is very good-looking.   ....
3 Dora liked the film *Billy Elliot*.   ....
4 Harry liked the film *Billy Elliot*.   ....
5 Dora and Harry think Scarlett Johansson is beautiful.   ....

4))) 1.46 **Listen again. Choose the correct options.**

1 Bobby Rickman is *an actor /* (*a celebrity look-alike*).
2 He's *thin / well-built*.
3 Dora and Harry's mother *knows / doesn't know* the film *Billy Elliot*.
4 Kelly Henshaw *is / isn't* an actress.
5 Kelly *is / isn't* a good look-alike.

Shopping

Speaking

1 🔊 **1.47** **Put the words in the right order. Then listen and check.**

1 this / much / How / T-shirt / is / ?
How much is this T-shirt?

2 you / Here / are / .
....

3 don't / want / thanks / I / it / .
....

4 got / cheap / any / Have / trainers / you / ?
....

5 you / Can / help / I / ?
....

6 's / cheap / That / very / !
....

2 🔊 **1.48** **Complete the conversation with these words and phrases. Then listen and check.**

~~awesome~~	have you got	help you
here you are	how much	I don't want them
they're		

Oliver Oh come on, Emma! Let's go! This shop is so boring!

Emma Don't be silly, Oliver! It's got some really cool things. What do you think of these jumpers? They're made of recycled T-shirts!

Oliver [1] *Awesome!*

Emma And these jeans are great!

Assistant Hi. Can I [2] .... ?

Emma I really like these jeans, but they're big. [3] .... any smaller ones?

Assistant [4] ....

Emma [5] .... are those?

Assistant Let me see ... [6] .... £45.

Emma Wow! They're expensive. [7] .... , thanks. All right, Oliver. Let's go.

Oliver At last!

Listening

3 🔊 **1.49** **Listen to the conversation. Are the sentences true (T), false (F) or don't know (DK)?**

1 Lucy and Tim are in a clothes shop. *F*

2 All the things in the shop are from Africa. ....

3 Tim buys a cheap T-shirt. ....

4 Lucy buys a cheap T-shirt. ....

4 🔊 **1.49** **Listen again. Complete the sentences with one word in each gap.**

1 The *notebooks* are made of recycled paper.

2 Children in .... make toys with wire and old bottle tops.

3 The things from South Africa are made of recycled paper and ....

4 Tim buys a cheap .... T-shirt.

5 Lucy likes a .... T-shirt.

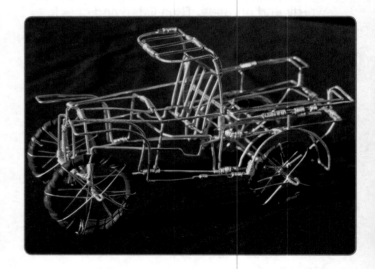

Offers

Speaking

1))) 1.50 **Listen to the conversations. Choose the correct options.**

1 A I don't feel well.
  B (Can I help you?) / Do you want some help?

2 A Can I get you / Do you want some water?
  B No, *please / thanks*. It's all right.

3 A I'm so tired today!
  B Can I get you / Do you want a cup of tea, Mum?
  A Oh, yes, *please / thanks*.

4 A I want to take part in a competition. I think I can win first prize.
  B *Go for it! / That's for sure!*

2))) 1.51 **Complete the conversation with these words and phrases. Then listen and check.**

all right	~~can I get you~~	please
some help	sure	thanks

Carla Oh … Oh … I feel terrible!
Matt What's wrong, Carla? ¹ *Can I get you* a glass of water?
Carla Yes, ² .... I don't feel well.
Suzie Listen, you're nervous. You'll be fine when you start singing. You'll win the competition.
Carla No, I can't sing in front of all those people!
Suzie Now come and change your clothes.
Carla No! I can't!
Suzie Do you want ³ .... ?
Carla No! … No, ⁴ .... Oh no!
Suzie What?
Carla I can't find my lucky charm. No, wait! It's ⁵ .... Here it is!
Suzie Carla! There isn't any time to change your clothes. Now go out there and sing. Good luck!
Matt Wow! Carla is really nervous.
Suzie That's for ⁶ .... !

Listening

3))) 1.52 **Listen to the conversation. Where are Lee and Zoe?**

a at the sports centre
b at Zoe's house
c at Lee's house

4))) 1.52 **Listen again. Are the sentences true (T), false (F) or don't know (DK)?**

1 Zoe feels tired.   *DK*
2 Lee offers her some water.   ....
3 Zoe thinks her mum's phone is at the sports centre.   ....
4 Lee offers to help Zoe find the phone.   ....
5 There's a phone in Zoe's sports bag.   ....

Apologising

Speaking

1 🔊 1.53 **Put the words in the correct order. Then listen and check.**

1 **A** Oh no! You've drunk all the juice!
B *I'm really sorry.*
('m / I / sorry / really)

2 **A** You've deleted an important email!
B ....
(an / accident / was / It)
A ....
(happen / These / things)

3 **A** Why do you always leave the TV on?
B ....
(It / again / happen / won't)
A That's OK.

4 **A** You burned the dinner!
B ....
(mean / I / to / didn't)
A ....
(right / It / all / 's)

2 🔊 1.54 **Complete the conversation with these words and phrases. Then listen and check.**

an accident	check out	don't
for goodness' sake	I didn't mean to	
~~really sorry~~	that's OK	

Sally Kevin, that music is very loud! I'm trying to do my homework.
Kevin Well, can I use your MP3 player, Sally?
Sally No! Don't touch it! Oh no! You've broken it!
Kevin I'm ¹ *really sorry*, Sally.
Sally ² .... Now be good.
Kevin Hey, ³ .... this website!
Sally Kevin! Go and play in your room! Oh no! You've dropped my laptop!
Kevin It was ⁴ ...., Sally.
Sally Oh, good. The laptop is all right.
Kevin ⁵ .... drop it.
Sally ⁶ .... worry. Now go away.
Kevin Can I play with these glass animals?
Sally No, you can't! ⁷ ....!
Go away, Kevin!
Kevin Oh, all right.

Listening

3 🔊 1.55 **Listen to the conversation. Who …**

1 is showing Alison photos? *Greg*
2 has been to Italy? ....
3 is bringing coffee? ....
4 offers to clean up? ....

4 🔊 1.55 **Listen again. Answer the questions.**

1 Where did Greg go on holiday this summer?
He went to Los Angeles.
2 Where did he go last year?
....
3 Where are the photos?
....
4 What happens to the coffee?
....
5 What is the bad news?
....

Reacting

Speaking

1))) 1.56 **Complete the conversations with one word in each gap. Then listen and check.**

1 A I passed all my exams.
  B Well *done*!

2 A I missed the bus again and I was late for dinner.
  B Oh .... It doesn't ....

3 A Our dog died last night.
  B .... a shame! That's .... !

4 A I'm going to travel around the world when I finish school.
  B Really? .... 's brilliant!

2))) 1.57 **Complete the conversation with these words and phrases. Then listen and check.**

brilliant	honestly	~~mate~~
oh well	what a	

Freya You know, everyone in our class is going away this summer.
Duncan Not everyone. I'll be here, and you and Bryan will be here, too. We can do things together.
Bryan Sorry, ¹*mate*. I'm going away this summer, too.
Freya ² .... Bryan! You didn't tell us.
Duncan Yes, ³ .... shame! Where are you going?
Bryan Well, my mum's an architect and she's going to Canada to design someone's house. So I'm going with her.
Freya That's ⁴ .... ! I want to go to Canada!
Duncan When are you coming back?
Bryan On the second of September – two days before school begins again.
Freya ⁵ .... Remember to send us emails, OK?
Bryan Yes, I promise.

Listening

3))) 1.58 **Listen to the conversations. Choose the correct options.**

1 Steve's news is *bad / neutral /* (*good*).
2 Mark's news is *bad / neutral / good*.
3 Ellen's news is *bad / neutral / good*.
4 Delia's news is *bad / neutral / good*.
5 Zak's news is *bad / neutral / good*.

4))) 1.58 **Listen again. Match the sentence beginnings (1–5) to the endings (a–e).**

1 Steve is phoning to tell his grandmother   *b*
2 Mark is phoning to tell his grandmother
3 Ellen is phoning to tell her grandmother
4 Delia is phoning to tell her grandmother
5 Zak is phoning to tell his grandmother

a he lost his job.
b he passed his exams with good marks.
c he has got a football match at the weekend.
d she didn't win a competition.
e she is going to take part in the Olympic Games.

Pronunciation

Consonants

Symbol	Example	Your examples
/p/	park	
/b/	big	
/t/	toy	
/d/	dog	
/k/	car	
/g/	good	
/tʃ/	chair	
/dʒ/	jeans	
/f/	film	
/v/	visit	
/θ/	three	
/ð/	they	
/s/	swim	
/z/	zoo	
/ʃ/	shop	
/ʒ/	television	
/h/	hot	
/m/	map	
/n/	notes	
/ŋ/	sing	
/l/	laptop	
/r/	room	
/j/	yellow	
/w/	watch	

Vowels

Symbol	Example	Your examples
/ɪ/	rich	
/e/	egg	
/æ/	rat	
/ɒ/	job	
/ʌ/	fun	
/ʊ/	put	
/iː/	eat	
/eɪ/	grey	
/aɪ/	my	
/ɔɪ/	boy	
/uː/	boot	
/əʊ/	note	
/aʊ/	now	
/ɪə/	hear	
/eə/	hair	
/ɑː/	star	
/ɔː/	north	
/ʊə/	tour	
/ɜː/	world	
/i/	happy	
/ə/	river	
/u/	situation	

Pronunciation practice

Unit 1   Verb endings: /s/, /z/, /ɪz/

1   )) 1.59   **Listen and repeat.**

dances	enjoys	hates	loses	loves
practises	runs	takes	writes	

2   **Complete the table.**

dances	enjoys	hates	loses	loves
practises	runs	takes	writes	

/s/	/z/	/ɪz/
....	....	....
....	....	....
....	....	....

3   )) 1.60   **Listen and check.**

Unit 2   Word stress in adjectives

1   )) 1.61   **Listen and repeat.**

boring	expensive	funny
romantic	rubbish	scary

2   **Circle the word with the correct stress.**
   1 <u>bor</u>ing   bor<u>ing</u>
   2 ex<u>pen</u>sive   expen<u>sive</u>
   3 fun<u>ny</u>   <u>fun</u>ny
   4 <u>ro</u>mantic   ro<u>man</u>tic
   5 <u>ru</u>bbish   rubb<u>ish</u>
   6 <u>sca</u>ry   scar<u>y</u>

3   )) 1.62   **Listen and check.**

Unit 3   Verb endings: /t/, /d/, /ɪd/

1   )) 1.63   **Listen. Write the correct pronunciation for the verbs: /t/, /d/ or /ɪd/.**
   Last night Jack <u>played</u> .... football and <u>watched</u> .... TV. He <u>started</u> .... his homework at 10 p.m.

2   **Complete the table.**

carried	loved	started
stopped	visited	watched

/t/	/d/	/ɪd/
....	....	....
....	....	....

3   )) 1.64   **Listen and check.**

Unit 4   *was* and *were*: strong and weak forms

1   )) 1.65   **Listen and repeat.**
   1 She was at home.
   2 Yes, you were.
   3 They were doing judo.
   4 We weren't happy.
   5 What were you doing?
   6 No, I wasn't.

2   )) 1.65   **Listen again. Tick the sentences that stress *was/wasn't* or *were/weren't*.**
   1 She was at home.
   2 Yes, you were.
   3 They were doing judo.
   4 We weren't happy.
   5 What were you doing?
   6 No, I wasn't.

3   )) 1.66   **Listen and check.**

Pronunciation

Unit 5 Intonation in questions and answers

1))) 1.67 **Listen and repeat.**

Has Nick got dark hair? ↗

No, he hasn't. ↘

2))) 1.68 **Listen. Draw ↗ or ↘.**

1 **A** Is she beautiful?

B Yes, she is.

2 **A** Has he got brown eyes?

B No, he hasn't.

3 **A** Is he well-built?

B No, he isn't.

3))) 1.68 **Listen again and repeat the questions and answers in Exercise 2.**

Unit 6 Silent letter *l*

1))) 1.69 **Listen and repeat.**
1 We talk every day.
2 Jack's a calm person.
3 I should drink more milk.
4 They always walk to school.
5 He drank half a bottle of water.

2 **Write the words with a silent letter *l*.**
1 ....
2 ....
3 ....
4 ....
5 ....

3))) 1.70 **Listen and check.**

Unit 7 *'ll*

1))) 1.71 **Listen and repeat.**
They play the guitar.
They'll play the guitar.

2))) 1.72 **Listen. Tick the sentences you hear.**
1 I'll buy all their albums.
I buy all their albums.
2 We dance every day.
We'll dance every day.
3 They'll enjoy the music.
They enjoy the music.

3))) 1.73 **Listen and repeat.**
1 They'll come later.
2 We'll see you in the park.
3 I'll give you the CD.
4 She'll record a new album.
5 It'll be exciting.

Unit 8 Syllables

1))) 1.74 **Listen and repeat.**
sea   island   waterfall

2 **Write the words in the correct group.**

| beach | continent | desert | lake | map |
| newspaper | rainforest | river | valley | |

●	● ●	● ● ●
sea	**island**	**waterfall**
....	....	....
....	....	....
....	....	....

3))) 1.75 **Listen and check.**

Unit 9 Schwa /ə/

1 **Underline the /ə/ sound in the words.**
1 She's a police officer.
2 The waiter served the other customers in the restaurant.

2))) 1.76 **Listen and repeat.**

Irregular Verb List

Verb	Past Simple	Past Participle
be	was/were	been
become	became	become
begin	began	begun
break	broke	broken
bring	brought	brought
build	built	built
buy	bought	bought
can	could	been able
catch	caught	caught
choose	chose	chosen
come	came	come
cost	cost	cost
cut	cut	cut
do	did	done
drink	drank	drunk
drive	drove	driven
eat	ate	eaten
feel	felt	felt
fight	fought	fought
find	found	found
fly	flew	flown
forget	forgot	forgotten
get	got	got
give	gave	given
go	went	gone/been
have	had	had
hear	heard	heard
hold	held	held
keep	kept	kept
know	knew	known

Verb	Past Simple	Past Participle
learn	learned/learnt	learned/learnt
leave	left	left
lose	lost	lost
make	made	made
mean	meant	meant
meet	met	met
pay	paid	paid
put	put	put
read /riːd/	read /red/	read /red/
run	ran	run
say	said	said
see	saw	seen
sell	sold	sold
send	sent	sent
sing	sang	sung
sit	sat	sat
sleep	slept	slept
speak	spoke	spoken
swim	swam	swum
take	took	taken
teach	taught	taught
tell	told	told
think	thought	thought
throw	threw	thrown
understand	understood	understood
wake	woke	woken
wear	wore	worn
win	won	won
write	wrote	written

My Assessment Profile Starter Unit

1 What can I do? Tick (✓) the options in the table.

⏪ = I need to study this again.   ⏸ = I'm not sure about this.   ▶ = I'm happy with this.   ⏩ = I do this very well.

		⏪	⏸	▶	⏩
Grammar (Student's Book pages 4 and 5)	• I can use all forms of *to be* in the Present simple. • I can use all forms of *have got* in the Present simple. • I can use all forms of *there is/are* in the Present simple. • I can use personal and object pronouns correctly. • I can use the possessive *'s*. • I can use possessive pronouns correctly.				
Vocabulary (SB pages 6 and 7)	• I can talk about places in a town. • I can talk about possessions. • I can talk about countries and nationalities. • I can talk about people.				
Reading (SB page 8)	• I can read and understand profiles of people on a social network.				
Writing (SB page 8)	• I can write my own profile for a social network.				
Speaking (SB page 9)	• I can ask someone for information about people and give information about myself.				
Listening (SB page 9)	• I can understand a conversation between friends.				

2 What new words and expressions can I remember?

words

....

expressions

....

3 How can I practise other new words and expressions?

record them on my MP3 player ☐   write them in a notebook ☐
practise them with a friend ☐   translate them into my language ☐

4 What English have I learned outside class?

	words	expressions
on the radio		
in songs		
in films		
on the internet		
on TV		
with friends		

My Assessment Profile Unit 1

1   **What can I do? Tick (✓) the options in the table.**

⏪ = I need to study this again.   ⏸ = I'm not sure about this.   ▶ = I'm happy with this.   ⏩ = I do this very well.

		⏪	⏸	▶	⏩
Vocabulary (Student's Book pages 10 and 13)	• I can talk about fifteen sports. • I can talk about sports equipment and places where people do sports.				
Reading (SB pages 11 and 16)	• I can read and understand an article about the Olympic Games and an article about the superstitions of famous athletes.				
Grammar (SB pages 12, 13 and 15)	• I can use the Present simple to talk about routines and habits and things that are true in general. • I can say what I like and don't like using *enjoy / hate / like / love / don't mind* + verb + *-ing*. • I can use adverbs of frequency to say how often something happens.				
Pronunciation (SB page 12)	• I can pronounce verb endings in the Present simple correctly.				
Speaking (SB pages 14 and 15)	• I can ask for opinions and give my opinion.				
Listening (SB page 16)	• I can understand a radio show.				
Writing (SB page 17)	• I can use punctuation correctly. • I can write a description of a sport.				

2   **What new words and expressions can I remember?**

words

....

expressions

....

3   **How can I practise other new words and expressions?**

record them on my MP3 player ☐   write them in a notebook ☐
practise them with a friend ☐   translate them into my language ☐

4   **What English have I learned outside class?**

	words	expressions
on the radio		
in songs		
in films		
on the internet		
on TV		
with friends		

My Assessment Profile Unit 2

1 What can I do? Tick (✓) the options in the table.

⏪ = I need to study this again. ⏸ = I'm not sure about this. ▶ = I'm happy with this. ⏩ = I do this very well.

		⏪	⏸	▶	⏩
Vocabulary (Student's Book pages 20 and 23)	• I can talk about twelve different types of films. • I can use adjectives.				
Reading (SB pages 21 and 26)	• I can read and understand a blog entry about a film museum, and an interview in a magazine with a film extra.				
Grammar (SB pages 22 and 25)	• I can use the Present continuous to talk about actions in progress. • I know when to use the Present simple and when to use the Present continuous.				
Pronunciation (SB page 23)	• I know where the stress is in adjectives.				
Speaking (SB pages 24 and 25)	• I can make suggestions and respond to them.				
Listening (SB page 26)	• I can understand an interview in the street.				
Writing (SB page 27)	• I can use linking words correctly. • I can write a film review.				

2 What new words and expressions can I remember?

words

....

expressions

....

3 How can I practise other new words and expressions?

record them on my MP3 player ☐   write them in a notebook ☐

practise them with a friend ☐   translate them into my language ☐

4 What English have I learned outside class?

	words	expressions
on the radio		
in songs		
in films		
on the internet		
on TV		
with friends		

My Assessment Profile Unit 3

1 What can I do? Tick (✓) the options in the table.

⏪ = I need to study this again.　⏸ = I'm not sure about this.　▶ = I'm happy with this.　⏩ = I do this very well.

		⏪	⏸	▶	⏩
Vocabulary (Student's Book pages 30 and 33)	• I can use fifteen words to talk about history. • I can use twelve words and expressions to talk about life events.				
Reading (SB pages 31 and 36)	• I can read and understand an advertisement for a tourist attraction and a biography of a famous person.				
Grammar (SB pages 32 and 35)	• I can use the Past simple of regular and irregular verbs to talk about the past.				
Pronunciation (SB page 32)	• I can pronounce verb endings in the Past simple correctly.				
Speaking (SB pages 34 and 35)	• I can ask for and give reasons.				
Listening (SB page 36)	• I can understand a history quiz.				
Writing (SB page 37)	• I can give information in the correct order in a biography. • I can write a biography.				

2 What new words and expressions can I remember?

words

....

expressions

....

3 How can I practise other new words and expressions?

record them on my MP3 player ☐ 　 write them in a notebook ☐

practise them with a friend ☐ 　 translate them into my language ☐

4 What English have I learned outside class?

	words	expressions
on the radio		
in songs		
in films		
on the internet		
on TV		
with friends		

My Assessment Profile Unit 4

1 What can I do? Tick (✓) the options in the table.

⏪ = I need to study this again.　⏸ = I'm not sure about this.　▶ = I'm happy with this.　⏩ = I do this very well.

		⏪	⏸	▶	⏩
Vocabulary (Student's Book pages 44 and 47)	• I can use twelve words and expressions to talk about breaking rules. • I can use eleven prepositions of movement.				
Reading (SB pages 45 and 50)	• I can read and understand a letter to a problem page in a magazine and a newspaper article about a crime.				
Grammar (SB pages 46 and 49)	• I can use the Past continuous to describe actions that were in progress at a particular time in the past. • I can use the Past simple and Past continuous with *when* and *while* to talk about an action that happened while another, longer action was taking place.				
Pronunciation (SB page 46)	• I can use the strong and weak forms of *was* and *were* correctly.				
Speaking (SB pages 48 and 49)	• I can show interest.				
Listening (SB page 50)	• I can understand an interview with the police.				
Writing (SB page 51)	• I can use sequencing words to show the order of events. • I can write a short story.				

2 What new words and expressions can I remember?

words

....　.......................　.......................　.......................　.......................

expressions

....　.......................　.......................　.......................　.......................

3 How can I practise other new words and expressions?

record them on my MP3 player ☐　　write them in a notebook ☐

practise them with a friend ☐　　translate them into my language ☐

4 What English have I learned outside class?

	words	expressions
on the radio		
in songs		
in films		
on the internet		
on TV		
with friends		

My Assessment Profile Unit 5

1 What can I do? Tick (✓) the options in the table.

⏪ = I need to study this again.　⏸ = I'm not sure about this.　▶ = I'm happy with this.　⏩ = I do this very well.

		⏪	⏸	▶	⏩
Vocabulary (Student's Book pages 54 and 57)	• I can talk about a person's physical appearance. • I can use twelve adjectives to describe a person's personality.				
Reading (SB pages 55 and 60)	• I can read and understand a website article about celebrity look-alikes and an article about two friends.				
Grammar (SB pages 56 and 59)	• I I can use comparative and superlative adjectives to compare people and things. • I can use the Present continuous to talk about future arrangements.				
Pronunciation (SB page 57)	• I can use the correct intonation in questions and answers.				
Speaking (SB pages 58 and 59)	• I can agree and disagree.				
Listening (SB page 60)	• I can understand different people talking about their personalities.				
Writing (SB page 61)	• I can put words in the correct order in a sentence. • I can write a description of a friend.				

2 What new words and expressions can I remember?

words

....

expressions

....

3 How can I practise other new words and expressions?

record them on my MP3 player ☐　　write them in a notebook ☐
practise them with a friend ☐　　translate them into my language ☐

4 What English have I learned outside class?

	words	expressions
on the radio		
in songs		
in films		
on the internet		
on TV		
with friends		

My Assessment Profile Unit 6

1 **What can I do? Tick (✓) the options in the table.**

⏪ = I need to study this again.   ⏸ = I'm not sure about this.   ▶ = I'm happy with this.   ⏩ = I do this very well.

		⏪	⏸	▶	⏩
Vocabulary (Student's Book pages 64 and 67)	• I can use twelve verbs to talk about the environment. • I can talk about six materials and six containers.				
Reading (SB pages 65 and 70)	• I can read and understand an article about organising a swap shop and an article about plastic bags and the environment.				
Grammar (SB pages 66, 67 and 69)	• I can use *going to* to talk about intentions for the future. • I can use *should* to make suggestions. • I can use *must* to talk about rules (obligations) and to give strong advice. • I can use *mustn't* to talk about things we are not allowed to do (prohibitions).				
Pronunciation (SB page 67)	• I can pronounce words with a silent letter / correctly.				
Speaking (SB pages 68 and 69)	• I can use and understand shopping expressions.				
Listening (SB page 70)	• I can understand a conversation about an exhibition in a museum.				
Writing (SB page 71)	• I can make my writing more interesting. • I can write an information leaflet.				

2 **What new words and expressions can I remember?**

words

....

expressions

....

3 **How can I practise other new words and expressions?**

record them on my MP3 player ☐   write them in a notebook ☐
practise them with a friend ☐   translate them into my language ☐

4 **What English have I learned outside class?**

	words	expressions
on the radio		
in songs		
in films		
on the internet		
on TV		
with friends		

My Assessment Profile Unit 7

1   **What can I do? Tick (✓) the options in the table.**

⏪ = I need to study this again.   ⏸ = I'm not sure about this.   ▶ = I'm happy with this.   ⏩ = I do this very well.

		⏪	⏸	▶	⏩
Vocabulary (Student's Book pages 78 and 81)	• I can talk about music, including six musical instruments and eleven types of music.				
Reading (SB pages 79 and 84)	• I can read and understand an article about the history and future of music and an article about teenagers in a choir.				
Grammar (SB pages 80 and 83)	• I can use *will* to talk about predictions about the future and to make offers. • I can use the first conditional to talk about something that will probably happen in the future as a result of another action or situation.				
Pronunciation (SB page 80)	• I can pronounce *'ll* correctly.				
Speaking (SB pages 82 and 83)	• I can make and respond to offers.				
Listening (SB page 84)	• I can understand an interview about a rock musical.				
Writing (SB page 85)	• I can use paragraphs correctly. • I can write a band profile.				

2   **What new words and expressions can I remember?**

words

....

expressions

....

3   **How can I practise other new words and expressions?**

record them on my MP3 player ☐   write them in a notebook ☐
practise them with a friend ☐   translate them into my language ☐

4   **What English have I learned outside class?**

	words	expressions
on the radio		
in songs		
in films		
on the internet		
on TV		
with friends		

My Assessment Profile Unit 8

1 **What can I do? Tick (✓) the options in the table.**

⏪ = I need to study this again.   ⏸ = I'm not sure about this.   ▶ = I'm happy with this.   ⏩ = I do this very well.

		⏪	⏸	▶	⏩
Vocabulary (Student's Book pages 88 and 91)	• I can use twelve words to talk about the natural world. • I can use twelve words to talk about camping.				
Reading (SB pages 89 and 94)	• I can read and understand articles about young adventurers.				
Grammar (SB pages 90 and 93)	• I can use the Present perfect to talk about past experiences at unspecified times and to ask about experiences.				
Pronunciation (SB page 91)	• I can recognise how many syllables there are in nouns and where the stress is.				
Speaking (SB pages 92 and 93)	• I can apologise and accept an apology.				
Listening (SB page 94)	• I can understand two friends talking about an adventure.				
Writing (SB page 95)	• I can begin and end an informal email correctly. • I can write an informal email.				

2 **What new words and expressions can I remember?**

words

....

expressions

....

3 **How can I practise other new words and expressions?**

record them on my MP3 player ☐   write them in a notebook ☐
practise them with a friend ☐   translate them into my language ☐

4 **What English have I learned outside class?**

	words	expressions
on the radio		
in songs		
in films		
on the internet		
on TV		
with friends		

My Assessment Profile Unit 9

1   What can I do? Tick (✓) the options in the table.

⏪ = I need to study this again.   ⏸ = I'm not sure about this.   ▶ = I'm happy with this.   ⏩ = I do this very well.

		⏪	⏸	▶	⏩
Vocabulary (Student's Book pages 98 and 101)	• I can use fourteen words to talk about jobs. • I can use ten adjectives to describe jobs.				
Pronunciation (SB page 98)	• I can pronounce the schwa sound /ə/ correctly.				
Reading (SB pages 99 and 104)	• I can read and understand an article about a theme park and an article about jobs for teenagers.				
Grammar (SB pages 100 and 103)	• I can use *a/an*, *some* and *any* correctly with countable and uncountable nouns. • I can use *many*, *much*, *a lot of*, *a few* and *a little* to talk about quantities. • I can use indefinite pronouns.				
Speaking (SB pages 102 and 103)	• I can react to bad news, neutral news and good news.				
Listening (SB page 104)	• I can understand a radio show about summer jobs.				
Writing (SB page 105)	• I can check my work correctly. • I can write a job questionnaire.				

2   What new words and expressions can I remember?

words

....

expressions

....

3   How can I practise other new words and expressions?

record them on my MP3 player ☐   write them in a notebook ☐
practise them with a friend ☐   translate them into my language ☐

4   What English have I learned outside class?

	words	expressions
on the radio		
in songs		
in films		
on the internet		
on TV		
with friends		

Pearson Education Limited,
Edinburgh Gate, Harlow
Essex, CM20 2JE, England
and Associated Companies throughout the world

www.pearsonelt.com

First published 2013
Sixth impression 2017

ISBN 978-1-4479-4360-0

Set in 10.5/12.5pt LTC Helvetica Neue Light
Printed in Slovakia by Neografia

Acknowledgements

The publisher would like to thank the following for their kind permission
to reproduce their photographs:

(Key: b-bottom; c-centre; l-left; r-right; t-top)

Alamy Images: adam james 108c, Adrian Sherratt 22c, Bushpilot 8l,
Hideo Kurihara 82cl, J.F.T.L IMAGES 71tl, Laura Ashley 71bc,
PicturesofLondon 6, Radius Images 38bl, 66tr, Richard Heyes 71c,
RichardBaker 42c; **Corbis**: Corbis Yellow 15b, 16b, 114br, I Love
Images / Alloy 60bl, Jutta Klee / Comet 32br, 115br, Koji Aoki / Aflo 9bl,
Kristy-Anne Glubish / Design Pics 61cl, Lawrence Manning / Spirit 8bc,
Ocean 10br, 58br, 66tl, 79br, 121br, Specialist Stock 57bl, Stan
Fellerman / Spirit 42tl, Tetra Images 7br; **Fotolia.com**: 7b, 7bc, 8r, 8b,
23bl, 29br, 42tr, 44bl, 48tl, 48tc, 51tc, 51tr, 51cr, 53tl, 53tc, 53tr, 53l,
53c, 53cl, 53cr, 53r, 53b, 53bl, 53bc, 53br, 71t, 71tr, 71cl, 71cr, 71r,
71bl, 71br, 74bl, 82c, 84bl, 104tr, 104cr, 104bc, 108tc, 109tc, 109tr,
109cr, 109bc, 110cr, 110bc, 111c, 111cr, 111cr, 111bc, 112tc, 112tr,
112c, 112cr, 112bc, 113br, 116bl, 126–135; **Getty Images**: AFP /
Jeff Haynes 8cr, Andersen Ross / Photodisc 42cr, 105cr, Ariel Skelley /
Blend Images 120br, Barbara Peacock / Photodisc 119br, Charles
Bowman / Photodisc 75bl, Christine Balderas / Photodisc 71tc,
Clerkenwell / the Agency Collection 81br, ColorBlind Images / Iconica
6tc, Comstock 48tr, Digital Vision 105tr, Fuse 110tc, Hill Street Studios /
Blend Images 35bl, i love images / Cultura 105c, Jason Hawkes /
The Image Bank 62br, Jena Cumbo / Photodisc 6tl, Jon Feingersh /
Blend Images 66tc, Juan Silva / Photodisc 51tl, Lisa Romerein / Riser
51cl, Martin Llado / Lonely Planet Images 109c, RL Productions / Digital
Vision 54bl, Siri Stafford / Stone+ 42r, Still Images 8br, Tariq Dajani /
The Image Bank 42tc, Westend 61 42br, Yellow Dog Productions /
Riser 104tc; **Lonely Planet Images**: Bethune Carmichael 118cr;
Pearson Education Ltd: 6t, 6cl, 6cr, 7t, 7tl, 7l, 7c, 7cl, 7r, 7bl, 19br,
26cl, 39bl, 42cl, 44cl, 44cr, 45br, 49bl, 59bl, 65br, 81bl, 104c, 108tr,
110tr, 111tc, 111tr, Trevor Clifford 71b; **Photolibrary.com**: Action Plus
8cl, fStop 8bl; **Rex Features**: Broadimage 67c, Nils Jorgensen 108bc,
WestEnd61 42l; **Sébastien Foucan**: Jon Lucas 14cl; **Shutterstock.
com**: versh 8c; **SuperStock**: Cusp 108cr, Eduardo Grund / age
fotostock 110c, Gallo Images 6br, i love images 33bl, 117br, Image
Source 79cr, Universal Images Group 30bl, View Pictures Ltd 6bl.

All other images © Pearson Education Limited

Cover image: *Front:* **Corbis**: Serge Kozak

Every effort has been made to trace the copyright holders and we
apologise in advance for any unintentional omissions. We would be
pleased to insert the appropriate acknowledgement in any subsequent
edition of this publication.

Illustrated by: Alfonso Abad pages 24, 34; Sonia Alins pages 13, 26,
37 (left), 53, 55, 71; Moreno Chiacchiera pages 25, 36, 37 (bottom
right), 39, 50, 68, 76, 106, 107; Paula Franco pages 4, 5, 12, 17, 18,
19, 27, 40, 41, 45, 63, 70, 73; Kate Rochester page 6.